STRENGTHENING
Your Marriage

Greg Laurie

STRENGTHENING
Your Marriage

Dana Point, California

STRENGTHENING Your Marriage

ISBN 0-9762400-4-1

Printed in the United States of America.

CONTENTS

INTRODUCTION 7

MARRIAGE: GOD'S IDEA 13

WHY IT'S HARD WORK 23

WHAT GOD SAYS TO HUSBANDS 35

WHAT GOD SAYS TO WIVES 47

THE INCREDIBLE POWER OF WORDS 59

STANDING STRONG AGAINST TEMPTATION 69

MARRIAGE IS A LIFELONG LIFESTYLE 83

NOTES 93

"He will restore, support, and strengthen you, and he will place you on a firm foundation. ... "

(1 Peter 5:10 NLT)

INTRODUCTION

As a pastor, I have conducted a lot of funerals and memorial services over the years. I have visited people who were literally on their deathbeds. From what I have witnessed, I can tell you that when your life comes to an end, there are two, maybe three things that will really matter to you. They are:

1. Faith
2. Family
3. Friends

First will be your faith, your relationship with God. I have heard more regrets from people who said they wished they had spent more time walking closely with God. They wished they had made more time for spiritual things. At the end of their lives, they have come to recognize the fact that they will stand before God Almighty. How sad it is when people realize they have squandered their lives.

Then comes family. "I wish I had been a better father," people say, or "I wish I had been a better mother." You will not be concerned about how much money you made, whether you had spent enough time at the office, or whether you had acquired enough possessions. You will have to leave all of your accomplishments and worldly goods behind. Sadly, we will spend so much time on that which does not really matter in the end, and in the process, we will neglect that which really does matter.

It is faith, family, and then friends that will be important when our lives draw to a close. These are things that we need to think about while there is still time. The Bible says, "Set your house in order" (Isa. 38:1). Those were the words of Isaiah the prophet to King Hezekiah when the king was close to death. I want to ask you something today: Is your house in order?

Sadly, thriving marriages are becoming more and more of an oddity in our culture. We see so many marriages that are falling apart. I wish that as Christians, we could just strike the word, "divorce," from our vocabularies, because God says that He hates it. So should we. It is true there are allowances for it in the Bible, and I will identify what those are in the pages ahead. I must also acknowledge there are times when some marriages simply aren't going to make it, because it does take a commitment on the part of two people.

But I can honestly say that in most of the situations in which I have seen a marriage fall apart, it could have been kept together if the husband and the wife simply would have done what the Bible says. I don't think people need to break apart as often as they do. That is why we need to get back to what God says.

Wedlock should be a padlock. Getting married should be locking up your union and throwing away the key as you determine to stand by the commitment you have made. If your marriage is miserable today, it is not the fault of the institution, but of the participants.

So before we get into the subject of how to make your marriage stronger, I want to ask you a couple of questions. I want you to think about this very carefully, because your responses to them will, in part, say a lot about the potential well-being of your marriage.

1. Do you believe the Bible is the Word of God?

This is important, because this is our basis. This is what I will be referring to throughout the rest of this book, and this is what it all will come down to. The Bible says in 2 Timothy 3:16, "All Scripture is inspired by God and is useful to teach us what is true and to make us realize what is wrong in our lives. It straightens us out and teaches us to do what is right. It is God's way of preparing us in every way, fully equipped for every good thing God wants us to do" (NLT). That includes marriage.

2. If you believe the Bible is the Word of God, are you going to obey it?

It is not enough to believe in the first principle if you are not going to apply the second. You can believe the Bible is the Word of God and not obey it. The devil believes the Bible is the Word of God. He hates it. He is opposed to it. Obviously, he doesn't live by it. But the Scripture says the demons believe and tremble (see James 2:19). So the question is, are you going to obey God's Word and apply it?

That is important, because Jesus made this statement at the end of the Sermon on the Mount. He said,

" 'Anyone who listens to my teaching and obeys me is wise, like a person who builds a house on solid rock. Though the rain comes in torrents and the floodwaters rise and the winds beat against that house, it won't collapse, because it is built on rock. But anyone who hears my teaching and ignores it is foolish, like a person who builds a house on sand. When the rains and floods come and the winds beat against that house, it will fall with a mighty crash.' " (Matt. 7:24–27)

This is a perfect picture of the family, because we build our homes on a foundation. The Scripture says, "Unless the Lord builds a house, they labor in vain that build it."

Is your marriage on the Rock or is it on the rocks? Is it built on Jesus Christ and His Word? Or, is it built on the shifting sand of human emotion? If it is built on the Rock, if it is built on Jesus Christ, then it means you hear these sayings of His, and you do them. If it is not built on Christ, then it means that you hear these sayings of His, but you don't do them. You may be going to church and attending Bible studies, but that doesn't necessarily mean you are doing what the Bible says. You need to obey it in your own life.

Notice that Jesus did not say *if* the rains and the floods come. Rather, He said *when* the rains and the floods come. Into every life a little rain must fall, and sometimes it will be a light drizzle, while other times it will be El Niño.

Every marriage will be tested. Every marriage will face difficulties. Every marriage will undergo attack. Therefore, we want to be ready because it is not a matter of if. It is only a matter of when.

In the pages ahead, we will be looking into God's Word to discover what He has to say about marriage and about our roles and responsibilities in this institution that He has established. We'll find out what we can do to strengthen our marriages and fortify them against those things that will come against it, both outwardly and inwardly.

If you're like me, you've probably joined a gym or started a new fitness program at one time or another in your life. You've learned that to reach your goals, you'll need to follow a prescribed program of diet and exercise. You've also learned that it is really hard work. But the end result is very reward-ing, isn't it? When you start to see the scales go down or notice your clothes fitting a little better than they did before, you're motivated to keep at it.

The same goes for building a strong marriage. There are time-tested principles from God's Word that you'll need to follow. There are old habits you'll need to change and new ones you'll need to learn. At times, it will be very hard work, and you might even feel like giving up. But the end result will be more rewarding than you can imagine—much more so than firming up and trimming down, as great as that might be.

At the end of each chapter, you'll find a section called "Strength Training," which is designed to help you begin putting what you've learned into practice. The section below it, called "Daily Supplements," includes recommended read-ings from my book, *Marriage Connections*. These give you more opportunity to add to your learning with more insights from God's Word on the subject of marriage.

In closing, I want to remind you that as we set out to strengthen our marriages, if we attempt it without God's help, we will utterly fail. It is only as we are filled with and are yielding to His Spirit that we can be the husbands and wives that He has called us to be.

I want to encourage you to take a few moments right now to stop and pray. Ask God to fill you with His Holy Spirit and to help you make a new commitment to strengthen your marriage.

Greg Laurie

And the Lord God said, "It is not good that man should be alone; I will make him a helper comparable to him." (Genesis 2:18)

MARRIAGE: GOD'S IDEA

Another book on marriage? That's what you might be thinking right now, and I more than understand. But yes, it is one more to add to the list. Frankly, I don't know that we can have too many. I have found over the years that as I have taught on the subject of marriage and the family, people really respond. That is why I have written this book—to encourage you in your marriage.

If you are not married yet, I am hoping that you will find some principles here that you can apply to make your new marriage strong and healthy. If you are in a strong and thriving marriage, I am hoping this book will strengthen you even more. But if your marriage is weak, perhaps even falling apart, it is my hope—and yes, prayer—that the principles found in this book will help to save your marriage.

Every marriage goes though changes as the years pass by. At the writing of this book, my wife and I have been married thirty-two years. It seems like yesterday when the eighteen-year-old Catherine Beatriz Martin walked down the aisle to marry a man who closely resembled Grizzly Adams. We have been together so long now that we can pretty much anticipate what the other will say and do (though more so her with me).

It's interesting how you treat one another as the years go by. Someone sent me an article called "The Seven Stages of a Married Cold" that illustrates this.

The first year: "Sugar dumpling, I'm really worried about my baby girl. You've got a bad sniffle and there's no telling about these things with all this strep going around. I'm putting you in the hospital this afternoon for a general checkup and a good rest. I know the food's lousy, but I'll be bringing your meals in from that gourmet restaurant you like so much."

The second year: "Listen darling, I don't like the sound of that cough. I've called the doctor and asked him to rush over here. Now you go to bed like a good girl, please, just for Daddy."

The third year: "Maybe you'd better lie down, Honey. Nothing like a little rest when you feel lousy. I'll bring you something. Have you got any canned soup?"

The fourth year: "Now look, dear, be sensible. After you've fed the kids, washed the dishes, and finished the floors, you'd better lie down."

The fifth year: "Why don't you take a couple of Tylenol?"

The sixth year: "I wish you would just gargle or something instead of sitting around all evening, barking like a seal."

The seventh year: "For Pete's sake, stop sneezing! Are you trying to give me pneumonia?"

Sometimes we take our mates for granted. So, how can we strengthen our marriages? Let's go back to the very beginning, to the very first married couple: Adam and Eve.

WHERE IT ALL BEGAN

I think sometimes we imagine the Garden of Eden almost like a fairy tale. We think of it as we would Camelot or Atlantis or Utopia. But the Bible gives us a historical account of real events that actually happened. We need to remember that Genesis, the first of the five books of Moses we know as the Pentateuch, was written to the people of Israel during the days of their wilderness wandering in the desert of Sinai. God was the eyewitness, and He gave these words to His servant, Moses, the author of Genesis.

There was really a place called Eden, and we are even given some specifics about where it was. Genesis 3:8 tells us, "The Lord God planted a garden eastward in Eden. … " Eden was located somewhere across the great Arabian Desert, toward the area of the present-day Tigris and Euphrates Rivers. We also read in Genesis 2:11 of places called Pishon and the land of Havilah. While we don't know for certain where these places were, the fact they are mentioned shows this was an actual geographical place. So here is the Garden of Eden. The whole world was beautiful and lush, but above all that, this garden was special. Think of all of the gorgeous places you have ever seen. Eden surpassed all of those. Eden was perfection.

In the midst of Eden was the Tree of Life. We find out later that the fruit of this tree, if eaten, could cause you to live forever. That is why, after Adam and Eve ate of the Tree of Knowledge of Good and Evil, they could not eat of the Tree of Life. God would not allow Adam and Eve to eat of the Tree of Life and live forever in their fallen state. We are told that, in the New Jerusalem, we will eventually have access to this tree. Revelation 22:2 says, "In the middle of its street, and on either side of the river, was the tree of life, which bore twelve fruits, each tree yielding its fruit every month. The leaves of the tree were for the healing of the nations."

So here was Adam, living in Eden. He had had everything that was pleasing to the eye (see Gen. 2:9). Adam's job description was to tend and keep the garden (v. 15), to serve and work. This does not mean that he was a glorified gardener, walking around with his tools and trimming the hedges. The Hebrew word used here for "keep" is a word that means, "discover its secrets." God was essentially saying, "Adam, I have put this here for you to enjoy. I want you to walk around and behold My glory and see My handiwork and just have a great time. I will be there to walk with you and have fellowship with you. But there is one thing, Adam. There is a tree over here that I have created, and I don't want you to eat from it." It was clear that God had established parameters. Then the Lord created animal life, and it was Adam's job to come up with names. Think of all the strange creatures in the world. Adam had to come up with a name for each of them. I wonder if he started running out of names after awhile. "Hmmm, this is a strange-looking animal. I don't know … how about hippopotamus?" Adam lived there in Eden, surrounded by the wonders of God's creation, yet there was still something missing in his life. Of course, Adam didn't know what it was, because that something actually was a someone who had not been created yet. But God knew. He said, " 'It is not good that man should be alone; I will make him a helper comparable to him' " (v. 18).

A MATCH MADE IN HEAVEN

We read again and again in Genesis 1 the phrase, "And God saw that *it was good*." But when God looked at Adam's loneliness, He said that it is not good. "It is not good that man should be alone." This is a very important question to be answered. Why did God bring woman to man? We find the answer in Genesis 2:18: "I will make him a helper comparable to him." This could be translated from the Hebrew, "Someone who assists another to reach fulfillment." It was used elsewhere in the Old Testament in reference to someone coming to the rescue of another. So Eve came to rescue Adam from his loneliness. God says that she is "comparable" to Adam, or corresponding to him.

This is important, because we live in a time in which our culture wants to say there are no differences between men and women, and that we program the differences into our children when they are young. The assertion is that if the social conditioning were simply changed, we would find that men and women are really the same. But that is simply not true. There was huge social experimentation in the 1960s and 70s, and the futility of this tampering with God's natural order was revealed. To say that men and women are different in practically every way is not to say that one is better than the other, But they are different. Both have been uniquely created in God's image.

In his book, *Love for a Lifetime*, Dr. James Dobson cites some of the physiological differences between men and women. He points out that the sexes differ in every cell of their bodies. For instance, a woman has greater constitutional vitality because of the chromosome difference. She usually outlives a man by three or four years, and in some cases, much longer. They also differ in their metabolism.

Women have lower metabolisms than men. Men and women also have different skeletal structures. Women have a shorter head, a broader face, a less protruding chin, shorter legs, and a longer trunk. Women have a larger stomach, liver, kidneys, and appendix, and have smaller lungs. In brute strength, men are 50 percent stronger than women.[1] We are different. God made us that way. So, "Vive la difference!"

Now we see the Lord bringing the woman to the man.

> And the Lord God caused a deep sleep to fall on Adam, and he slept; and He took one of his ribs, and closed up the flesh in its place. Then the rib which the Lord God had taken from man He made into a woman, and He brought her to the man. And Adam said: "This is now bone of my bones and flesh of my flesh; she shall be called Woman, because she was taken out of Man." (Gen. 2:21–23)

So, after another glorious day in the garden, Adam fell into a deep sleep. Much to his surprise, when he awoke there was Eve! Adam enthusiastically exclaims, "This is now bone of my bones and flesh of my flesh." Hebrew experts tell us that Adam's reaction was one of thrilling, joyous astonishment. He takes a nap, wakes up, sees Eve, and says, "Yes! This is good!" She is perfect in every way for Adam. A partner. Someone to share his life with.

MARRIAGE: GOD'S DESIGN

So God brings Adam and Eve together and establishes marriage: "Therefore shall a man leave his father and his mother, and shall cleave unto his wife: and they shall be one flesh" (v. 24 KJV). It is interesting to note that Jesus referenced this same statement in the New Testament. When the Pharisees came to Him and said, " 'Is it lawful for a man to divorce his wife for just any reason?' " (Matt. 19:3), Jesus told them, " 'Have you not read that He who made them at the beginning "made them male and female," ' " (v. 4). Jesus then referred to this verse, " ' "For this reason a man shall leave his father and mother and be joined to his wife, and the two shall become one flesh"?'" (v. 5).

Long before there was a nation or a government, a school or even a church, there was a man and woman brought together to be husband and wife. So modern culture began with the family. And if we tamper with God's original plan, we do so at our own peril.

It has been said, "A family can survive without a nation, but a nation cannot survive without the family." This verse also provides some essential truths regarding God's design for marriage. In fact, two words sum it up: leaving and cleaving. First you must leave. Then you must cleave.

Marriage begins with a leaving—a leaving of all other relationships. The closest relationship outside of marriage is specified here, which is the relationship of a child to his parents. This implies that if it is necessary to leave your father and mother, then all lesser ties must be broken, changed, or left behind. You leave all other relationships, at least in their present state. Of course, you are still a son or a daughter to your parents, but it is different now because you have been joined to your spouse. Your relationship with your parents has changed. A new family has been established. A man's primary commitment, once he is married, is to his wife, and her primary commitment is to him.

But what happens in many marriages is this process of leaving never takes place. One or both parties think, "If things don't work out, I can always run home to my parents," or, "If things don't work out, I'm going to run to my old friends and hang out with them." People who think this way never have really left other relationships and haven't chosen to cleave to their spouse. Husbands, your best friend and closest confidant in life needs to be your wife. Wives, the same needs to be true for you. It is good to have other friends, but there should only be one best friend in your life, and it should be your spouse.

It becomes especially dangerous when a wife has male friends other than her husband, and a husband has female friends other than his wife. You see, the problem is that you start bonding with these people. It can easily lead to greater friendship, and even intimacy, and ultimately outright adultery.

Most adulterous relationships, especially in the case of women, did not begin with sexual attraction. They began because a woman felt that her husband wasn't giving her the attention she wanted and wasn't spending time with her. So, she developed a friendship with a man. "We're just friends. It's nothing more. He understands me. I understand him. We encourage one another. We pray together. We read the Bible together." These can easily become famous last words. The same goes for men. Husbands, make your wife your best friend. Wives, make your husband your best friend. Cultivate the friendship in your marriage. After all, that was God's master plan for marriage from the very beginning: companionship.

Listen to what God says in Malachi 2:14: "The Lord has been witness between you and the wife of your youth, with whom you have dealt treacherously; yet she is your companion and your wife by covenant." Notice the words, "companion and wife." That word, "companion," could be translated from the Hebrew to say, "One you are united with in thoughts, goals, plans, and efforts." Is that a good description of your present relationship with your spouse?

Then in 1 Peter 3, we read, "Husbands, likewise, dwell with them with understanding, giving honor to the wife, as to the weaker vessel, and as being heirs together of the grace of life, that your prayers may not be hindered" (v. 7). The word Peter used for "dwell" means, "to be aligned to or to give maintenance to." So to put it all together, God is saying, "Be aligned to your wife. Give regular maintenance to your relationship. Be united with her in thoughts, goals, plans, and efforts." Friendship, companionship, and closeness: these form the foundation of marriage.

So first you must leave. Every other relationship in your life must work in proportion with the relationship between you and your spouse. There is a place for buddies. There is a place for hobbies. There is a place for your career. But you shouldn't let anything get in the way of your relationship with your spouse. That is all a part of the leaving process.

But then Scripture says there must be a cleaving. It is no use leaving unless you are willing to spend a lifetime cleaving. The word used in Genesis 2:24 for "cleave" means, "to adhere to, to stick to, to be attached by some strong tie." You might be thinking, "That's me, all right. I'm stuck." But that is not what this word means. In the verb form, it speaks of something that is done aggressively, a determined action. It is not talking about merely being stuck together, but it is the idea of holding on to something. In other words, it is not that you are just held to something, like a fly on flypaper, wanting to get loose. It is something you are willfully holding on to.

For example, if you were walking along the edge of a cliff, suddenly lost your footing, went over the side, and grabbed a branch, you are holding on to that branch because it is something you want to do. It is something you do by will, because your life depends upon it. That is the idea of the word, "cleave," used here. It is not that you are "stuck" to your spouse, but you are holding on—not passively, but aggressively. This is what needs to happen in our marriages. We need to hang on to each other. There are so many pressures on us to be pulled apart. So there needs to be a determined action to hold on to one another and to stay away from anything or anyone that would separate you. That is the idea here in the Hebrew.

When you come to the New Testament use of the same word in the Greek language, it means, "to cement together, to stick like glue, or to be welded together so the two cannot be separated without serious damage to both."

Therefore, we must periodically take stock in our lives and ask ourselves, "Is there any relationship or pursuit in which I'm currently involved that would put distance between my mate and me? Is this thing that I am doing drawing us together or is it driving us apart? Will it build our relationship up or will it tear it down?"

It is not always the big things that bring a marriage down; it is often the small things. Certainly there are the big issues in a marriage, such as unfaithfulness or abuse. These can destroy a marriage quickly. But it is the little things that often bring the marriage down. As Song of Solomon says, it is "the little foxes that spoil the vines" (2:15). In a marriage, it can be a matter of neglecting the principle of leaving and cleaving. When there is an unwillingness to hold on tightly to your spouse, your marriage can begin to weaken. Problems can develop. The affection you should have for your mate can be transferred to someone else instead. So cleave to your spouse, recognizing that all other relationships must be secondary.

Concentrate on leaving and cleaving. All other relationships must be evaluated in the light of your relationship with your spouse. Make him or her your best friend. Start communicating with each other like never before. Hold on to each other instead of thinking, "We're married. I suppose we'll stick together." Work on your marriage. Seek to make it better. And as you aggressively do your part, following the counsel of Scripture, God will do His part, and He will bless your home.

Leave and cleave: these are two key words in a successful marriage.

STRENGTH TRAINING

- *Are there any relationships or pursuits in your life today that take precedence over your relationship with your husband or wife? Ask God to reveal any changes you need to make, and ask Him to help you follow through with those changes.*

DAILY SUPPLEMENTS

- *Each day this week, read one of the following selections from* Marriage Connections: *"Vive la Difference," "Something's Missing," "Adam's Rib," "Your Best Friend," "The Need to Leave," "Sticking Together or Just Plain Stuck?" and "Finding Fulfillment."*

Lead a life worthy of your calling, for you have been called by God. Be humble and gentle. Be patient with each other, making allowance for each other's faults because of your love. Always keep yourselves united in the Holy Spirit, and bind yourselves together with peace. (Ephesians 4:1–3 NLT)

2

WHY IT'S HARD WORK

God wants to bless our marriages. After all, it was God who designed marriage. He originated it, He has uniquely established it, and He has given it as a blessing to humanity.

Because of this, Satan wants to destroy our marriages. There is no question that he has set his sights on the family, and there is nothing that would give him greater delight than to see it destroyed—especially Christian families. That is why we want to do everything we can to draw a line around our homes and say, "This belongs to the Lord. We are going to do it God's way, and we are going to build our marriage on God's principles."

When it comes to these principles, two operative words stand out, as we saw in the previous chapter: *leave and cleave.* This is God's order for a man and a woman: leaving and cleaving, or severing and bonding, or loosing and securing, or departing from and attaching to (see Gen. 2:24, Matt. 19:5–6, Mark 10:7–9). First, you leave. This means that all other relationships are impacted. All lesser ties must be broken, changed, or left behind. Marriage affects everything.

But let's remember why God causes a man and a woman to leave in the first place. It is so they can cleave, so they can become one flesh. Why did God bring man and woman together? Because He said, " 'It is not good that man should be alone … ' " (Genesis 2:18). Now it is true that the husband and wife are going to be lovers and will probably be parents. But first and foremost, they are to be friends. This is where so many marriages are hurting today. A husband and wife are no longer friends. They have lost the intimacy. They have lost the closeness. Show me a marriage where this intimacy is breaking down and this closeness is not taking place, and I will show you a marriage that is ultimately headed for trouble. On the other hand, show me a marriage where this principle is operative and intact, and I will show you a marriage that can weather the storms that will come its way.

LOOKING OUT FOR NUMBER ONE

But tragically, marriages are falling apart at a record pace. And what is especially disheartening is to see how divorces are happening in the church. Even worse, they are rarely based on biblical grounds. Of course, we live in a culture that is, in many ways, openly hostile to the family itself. Activists do everything in their power to undermine and redefine what marriage and family really are.

It is hammered into our lives through every form of media. We see it in the magazines, television programs, and movies. We hear it in the music. What is that message? To seek your own happiness. Whatever cost is involved is acceptable. We are essentially told to believe, "Everything revolves around me. I am the only thing that matters."

Concepts like sacrifice, selflessness, and keeping one's commitment are rarely heard of today, and we carry this same, selfish, "me-first" mentality into our marriages. We say, "I will marry you so you can make me a happy person. As long as you fulfill me and meet my needs, I will stay with you—that is unless someone better or more interesting comes along." Now, we might not come right out and verbalize that, but judging by the way many people act and behave today, it is reality.

Understand what I am saying here. I am not suggesting that you cannot be happy and fulfilled in a marriage. What I am saying is that if you go into marriage with the sole expectation of your spouse meeting your needs and without any real concern about your meeting theirs, you will be disappointed. The right motive would be wanting to marry someone so you can make him or her happy, so you can meet their needs, and so you can bring them fulfillment. That should be the motive. Yet self-obsession is so prevalent in our society today. In fact, the Bible tells us it would be paramount in the last days, a time in which I believe we are now living. According to 2 Timothy 3:1–2, "In the last days perilous times will come: For men will be *lovers of themselves*, lovers of money, boasters, proud, blasphemers, disobedient to parents, unthankful, unholy, unloving, unforgiving, slanderers, without self-control, brutal, despisers of good, traitors, headstrong, haughty, lovers of pleasure rather than lovers of God…" (vv. 1–4, emphasis mine).

You might be thinking, "Wait a second. I thought we needed to love ourselves. I thought the biggest problem in our culture was a lack of self-love. I thought that all of the problems of our culture could be traced to low self-esteem and poor self-image." Yet the Bible says that one of the signs of the last days, a sinful trait, will be that people will love themselves more than they love God. You see, it is because of our self-love; it is because of our fixation and obsession with self, that we have many of the problems in our culture today. In our entertainment-saturated society, we are living in an altered state of reality. We live with illusions of what life should be: the fantasy of the perfect romantic and sexual relationship, the fantasy of the perfect husband or the perfect wife, the fantasy of the perfect lifestyle. Yet it is a nonexistent reality that we chase after. And when life doesn't measure up to what we think it should, we simply say, "I must go and search for it somewhere else." This often includes bailing out on a marriage.

A HIGHER CALLING

As Christians, we must abandon this unbiblical and destructive type of thinking, because God has called us, as His children, to a different standard. He has called us to a higher level of living, a new way of thinking and behaving. Ephesians 4:1–2 tells us, "Walk worthy of the calling with which you were called, with all lowliness and gentleness, with longsuffering, bearing with one another in love. … "

As Christians, we cannot think as this world thinks or act as it acts. God says, " 'Come out from among them and be separate' " (2 Cor. 6:17). In Romans 12:2 we read, "Don't let the world around you squeeze you into its own mould, but let God re-make you so that your whole attitude of mind is changed" (*PHILLIPS*). So, selfishness must be abandoned, and in its place, we must find a new, selfless, God-honoring life in which we put God's Word above our own desires. If we want our marriages to be strong, then we must place obedience to God and the needs of our spouse above our own.

While our culture tells us that self-esteem is the most important thing, the Bible tells us to esteem others better than ourselves: "Let nothing be done through selfish ambition or conceit, but in lowliness of mind let each *esteem others* better than himself. Let each of you look out not only for his own interests, but also for the interests of others" (Phil. 2:3–4, emphasis mine). If every married couple did this alone, our homes would be transformed overnight. If you put the needs of your wife or husband above your own and thought of their happiness and their fulfillment above yours, it would radically change your home.

WHAT STARTED IT ALL

This, of course, not only flies in the face of cultural norms, but also opposes basic human nature. It all goes back to Eden. Let's take a look at Genesis 3:

> Now the serpent was more cunning than any beast of the field which the Lord God had made. And he said to the woman, "Has God indeed said, 'You shall not eat of every tree of the garden'?" And the woman said to the serpent, "We may eat the fruit of the trees of the garden; but of the fruit of the tree which is in the midst of the garden, God has said, 'You shall not eat it, nor shall you touch it, lest you die.' " Then the serpent said to the woman, "You will not surely die. For God knows that in the day you eat of it your eyes will be opened, and you will be like God, knowing good and evil." So when the woman saw that the tree was

good for food, that it was pleasant to the eyes, and a tree
desirable to make one wise, she took of its fruit and ate.
She also gave to her husband with her, and he ate. Then
the eyes of both of them were opened. … (vv. 1–7)

Eve was at the wrong place at the wrong time, listening to
the wrong voice, which led her to do the wrong thing. Adam
soon joined her, and when confronted by God for an explana-
tion of his disobedience, offered the first excuse recorded in
human history. Adam said, "The woman whom You gave to
be with me, she gave me of the tree, and I ate" (v. 12). I don't
know what Adam might have emphasized in this response
to God.

It could have come down to what word he emphasized.
For instance, if Adam said, "It's the *woman* you gave me,"
he was placing the blame on Eve, not himself. On the other
hand, if Adam said, "It's the woman *You* gave me," he would
have been placing the blame on God himself. Whatever the
case, it was a lame excuse, as Adam was fully responsible for
his own actions.

Eve did not fare much better as she tried to blame it all on
Satan, as though she had nothing to do with it. "The serpent
deceived me, and I ate" (v. 13). Loose paraphrase: "It's not
my fault; the devil made me do it."

There was no excuse, however. Adam and Eve both crossed
the line, knowing it was the wrong thing to do. As a result
of that sin, a curse came upon humanity, and we still feel
its repercussions to this very day. As a result of this curse, a
number of things entered into the human race, starting with
death. Up to this point, Adam and Eve would not have died
or faced disease or the aging process. But because of their
sin, the curse of sickness, a limited life span, and the ultimate
termination of life on Earth began.

Remember, God said, "But of the tree of the knowledge of
good and evil you shall not eat, for in the day that you eat of it
you shall surely die" (Genesis 2:17). They ate of it. And death
entered the human race.

Also part of this curse was pain in childbirth: "To the
woman He said: 'I will greatly multiply your sorrow and your

conception; in pain you shall bring forth children …' " (Gen. 3:16). The wonderful joy of giving birth to a child would now be impacted by physical pain. I was present at the birth of both of our children. We went through the natural childbirth classes. Cathe worked on her breathing techniques to alleviate the pain of contractions, and I was her "coach." She did a great job bringing our children into this world. We have two wonderful sons, yet Cathe went through all of the pain. Let me just say that I am thankful this part of the curse was not on men. I surely would not have held up as well as she did.

But we men also have our part of the curse to bear, which is strenuous work. Prior to his fall into sin, Adam's job was primarily to enjoy the glory and splendor of what God had made. But now he would have to labor hard and long to work and to make a living. God said to Adam,

> "Cursed is the ground for your sake; in toil you shall eat of it all the days of your life. Both thorns and thistles it shall bring forth for you, and you shall eat the herb of the field. In the sweat of your face you shall eat bread till you return to the ground, for out of it you were taken; for dust you are, and to dust you shall return." (Gen. 3:17–19)

Finally, there is something significant resulting from this curse that affects our marriages to this day: strife and selfishness. After Eve sinned in the garden, which was a result of her disobedience to God and her failure to consult with Adam about the serpent's temptation, the Lord had something very important to say to her: "Your desire shall be for your husband, and he shall rule over you" (v. 16). Again, it is important that we keep in mind when we read this verse, that this statement was part of the curse. Looking at the words in the original language will help us understand a dynamic that is the cause of the tension between men and women to this very day and the reason there is a battle of the sexes.

The word that God used for "desire" is the same word also used in Genesis 4—the identical Hebrew word—and comes from a root word that means, "to compel, to impel, to urge, or to seek control over." Using the same word in Genesis 4:7, the

Lord warned Cain, "Sin lies at the door. And its *desire* is for you, but you should rule over it" (emphasis mine). God was essentially saying, "Cain, sin wants to control you, but you must control sin." In light of this close contextual meaning of the word, "desire," the curse on Eve was that woman's desire would be to henceforth usurp the place of her husband's headship, and in other words, she would want to rule her husband.

At this point, men who are reading this are probably thinking, "Greg, this is good stuff! I like this. Hallelujah! Preach it to the women." But hold on, guys. This is a double-edged sword, because the word that is used in this verse for "rule" is a word that means, "to subdue, to put under your feet." This is a part of the curse too. It was not something God was advocating; it was something that God was acknowledging as a result of sin. In other words, it was speaking of a new kind of authoritarianism that was not in God's original plan for man's headship. With Adam and Eve's sin and the curse that followed came the distortion of woman's proper submissiveness and man's proper authority. This is where male chauvinism and women's liberation had its beginning. Woman has a sinful inclination to usurp the authority of her husband, and man has a sinful inclination to put his wife under his feet. Both are equally wrong before God.

EQUAL STANDING, DIFFERENT FUNCTIONS

Some today will assert that the Bible is a sexist book. Yet anyone who makes a statement like this demonstrates an obvious ignorance of Scripture and biblical culture. We must examine what the Bible is really saying and dispel this ridiculous thinking. If anything, the Bible and its message liberated women. The apostle Paul, who has been wrongly labeled a chauvinist by some, said, "Husbands, love your wives, just as Christ also loved the church and gave Himself for her … " (Eph. 5:25). That was radical stuff for the time in which Paul was living. Telling a husband to love his wife as Christ loved the church, to give himself for her—that was quite different from what husbands had heard up to that point. In Roman culture, women were treated as possessions, not partners in life. In the twisting of Scripture, even in the Jewish culture of the day, a man could divorce his wife for practically any reason.

So let's not take this secular thinking of today and try to attach it to Scripture. The Bible gives us the truth about how we are to live and how we are to function. Men and women are equal before God, but we are different. Our roles are different as well. When we fail to see that, we make a big mistake. God has wired men and women in different ways. Obviously, we have equal access to God, but He uses us in different ways. So instead of being upset about that, we should celebrate it and rejoice in it, because it all works out in His plan and His balance.

But you see, the problem with most marriages today is not money or careers or children or in-laws. The problem with most marriages today could be summed up in one word: self. We love to blame this thing or that thing for our difficulties in marriage. But the problem is ourselves. James asks, "What is causing the quarrels and fights among you? Isn't it the whole army of evil desires at war within you?" (James 4:1 NLT). We bring these problems into our marriages because of our natural, sinful bent and our natural orientation toward ourselves, which often leads to such inane sayings as, "I am no longer happy in my marriage," "I need my own space," "My mate is no longer meeting my needs," and "I am going to go find myself." This ridiculous, selfish orientation is what destroys so many marriages.

WHERE STRENGTH COMES FROM

While it is true that selfishness is part of human nature, it is not true that we're beyond the hope of changing. The Bible tells us, "If anyone is in Christ, he is a new creation; old things have passed away; behold, all things have become new" (2 Cor. 5:17). God is telling us that we have a new nature, and we are to live by new standards. And, He has given us new power to do it with.

Ephesians 5 has much to say to husbands and wives, and

we will examine these things more closely in the chapters to come. But for now, I want to take a look at some introductory verses that are often forgotten when we talk about the Christian family:

> And do not be drunk with wine, in which is dissipation; but be filled with the Spirit, speaking to one another in psalms and hymns and spiritual songs, singing and making melody in your heart to the Lord, giving thanks always for all things to God the Father in the name of our Lord Jesus Christ, submitting to one another in the fear of God. (vv. 18–21)

In the verses following the passage above, we read that wives are to submit to their husbands and husbands are to love their wives as Christ loved the church. But before a word is spoken about any of these things, God says, "Be filled with the Spirit." You see, we need to realize that we can't do this in our own strength. We need to look at these commands in Scripture and understand that a husband cannot love his wife as Christ loves the church and a wife cannot effectively submit to her husband as unto the Lord without the help of the Holy Spirit. Recognizing this, God says, "Be filled with the Spirit." Before a word is mentioned about the specific roles of the husband and wife, God puts forth His prerequisite: "Be filled with the Spirit." In the original language, this statement is a command. God is not saying, "Would you mind, as a personal favor to Me, if you have time, please, be filled with the Spirit." God is saying, "I command you to be filled with the Spirit."

There's another thing we need to know about this phrase, "Be filled with the Spirit." It speaks of a continuous action. It could be translated from the Greek, "Be constantly filled over and over again with the Holy Spirit." Let's say that you went out and bought a new car. You were told this car would run 100,000 miles, easy, or maybe 200,000 miles. "That's great," you think. So you drive it off the lot. You have been driving it for about a week with no problems. Then one day, it sputters and comes to a standstill. "That salesperson lied to me," you're thinking. Then on your dashboard you notice a little red light and an arrow pointing toward the letter "E." You are out of fuel. You don't need to take the car back and trade it in. You just need to get a refill. You just need to go to the gas station.

In the same way, your marriage can be humming along and things can be going great. Then all of the sudden, you find yourself chugging rather than humming. Maybe you've thought, "I need to trade this old model in on a new one." No. You just need a refill. Did you know that God gives refills? You just pull in and say, "Lord, fill me with the Spirit. Fill me again." Each and every day you say, "Lord, I need to be empowered by and filled with your Holy Spirit. I am completely dependent upon You."

IT'S THAT WORD AGAIN

What does the filling of the Spirit help me to do? We find the answer a few verses later: "Submitting to one another in the fear of God" (Eph. 5:21). Have you ever noticed that verse before? We men like to say, "Wife, dear, the Bible says right here in Ephesians 5:22, 'Wives, submit to your own husbands, as to the Lord.' " But do we ever notice the phrase in verse 21 that reads, "Submitting to one another in the fear of God"? This is very important. We like to point out the verses about men leading and women submitting. But we also need to remember that God tells us both as husbands and wives to submit to one another in the fear of God.

Of course, the word, "submit," is not a popular word in our narcissistic, me-first culture. Submitting is equated with giving up your rights. "I won't be a doormat for anyone," we say. But God says, "Don't be drunk with wine, because that will ruin your life. Instead, let the Holy Spirit fill and control you. … And further, you will submit to one another out of reverence for Christ" (Eph. 5:18, 21 NLT). In other words, you need God's help to do this. But perhaps the confusion arises because we don't even understand what it means to submit to someone in the first place. To submit means, "to get in order under something." In a military sense, it means to rank beneath or under. So what this is saying to a husband is that a husband's submission to his wife does not mean that he is abdicating his responsibility of leadership in the home. Instead, he helps his wife to bear her burdens and carry her cares. He is always ready to meet her needs and sacrifice his own desires for what helps to fulfill those needs. He says, "I am going to support her. I am going to get under her and help her." But then she is doing the same for him. That is what submitting to one another means.

We are all submitting at some point. Wives are called to submit to the loving leadership of their husbands. Husbands are to bow to the needs of their wives. But it comes down to obedience to God. We do these things out of reverence for the Lord, because this is God's order. We need to do it His way. While there are distinctions in the roles of husbands and wives, it is not a matter of being greater or lesser or superior or inferior. They are each different, but significant, roles. In the next two chapters, we will look at what God says specifically to husbands and wives. It is significant. But before we do, let's take one more look at what we've learned.

First, God has told us what the problem is. Men have a natural desire to rule over their wives. Women have a natural desire to control their husbands. They are both sinful tendencies, and they are both wrong.

Second, God has said that we can't, in our own strength, do what we need to. We need to be filled with the Spirit.

Third, we need to submit to one another in the fear of God. We need to put the needs of our spouses above our own.

If you were to concentrate on these three things alone, you could have one of the happiest marriages around. But there is a lot more God has to say to us.

STRENGTH TRAINING

- *Have you ever asked God to fill you with His Holy Spirit? Or, have you asked Him for a refill lately? Stop and ask Him to fill, or refill, you with His Spirit today and to empower you to be the husband or wife He has called you to be.*

DAILY SUPPLEMENTS

- *Each day this week, read one of the following selections from* Marriage Connections: *"The Battle of the Sexes," "Time for a Refill," "Equal Standing, Different Functions," "Radical Love," "Active Love," "Pursuing Kindness," and "Till Death Do Us Part."*

*Therefore do not be unwise, but understand
what the will of the Lord is.
(Ephesians 5:17)*

WHAT GOD SAYS TO HUSBANDS

A man was walking along a Southern California beach and spotted an unusual-looking bronze object lying in the sand. He picked it up and began to dust it off, when all of the sudden, a genie appeared. The genie told him, "Master, I will grant you one wish."

"One wish?" the man asked. "What happened to three wishes?"

"With the economy and everything, we've had to cut back," the genie told him.

"OK, I'll tell you what," the man said. "I love Hawaii, but I don't like to fly. If you could build me a highway from California to Hawaii so that I could drive there, that would be great. So that is my one wish. I want a highway from California to Hawaii."

"Give me a break!" the genie exclaimed. "There is no way that I could do that. Think of the logistics involved. It is absolutely impossible. You'll need to choose something else."

The man thought about it for awhile. "OK, I think I have it now," he said. "I don't understand women at all, especially my wife. My wish is that I would be able to understand women from this point forward."

The genie paused for a moment, then turned to the man and said, "Did you want that highway two lanes or four?"

I wish I could share with you the key to understanding your wife, but having been married thirty-two years, I can honestly say that I have no idea. Even though we husbands might have a hard time understanding our wives sometimes, we still are to love them (and they can be so lovable). Every marriage, however, will face difficulties and challenges—even good marriages. In fact, sometimes this is what makes a good marriage. As we come through those difficulties, we learn how to bend, be flexible, and most importantly, how to love and forgive.

But we need to ask ourselves, "Am I as a husband doing my part in the marriage?" The question is not whether your wife is doing her part. The question is, are you doing yours? A failure to understand and apply the specific roles and responsibilities given to the husband and wife is the reason for the breakdown of so many marriages today. Do you know what your responsibilities are? Scripture is quite clear on the subject. In fact, I will venture to say that the bulk of the responsibility for the success of the marriage, in my opinion, rests squarely on the shoulders of the man. Instead of being the spiritual leaders and initiators that God has called us to be, too many men in Christian marriages today are at best passive and at worst a hindrance to the spiritual growth of the family. We are not being the leaders we ought to be. Many marriages are in trouble today because men are unwilling to obey God's commands to them.

TAKE THE LEAD

So what are these commands? Let's look at some of them in Ephesians 5.

> Husbands, love your wives, just as Christ also loved the church and gave Himself for her, that He might sanctify and cleanse her with the washing of water by the word, that He might present her to Himself a glorious church, not having spot or wrinkle or any such thing, but that she should be holy and without blemish. So husbands ought to love their own wives as their own bodies; he who loves his wife loves himself. For no one ever hated his own flesh, but nourishes and cherishes it, just as the Lord does the church. For we are members of His body, of His flesh and of His bones. "For this reason a man shall leave his father and mother and be joined to his wife, and the two shall

become one flesh." This is a great mystery, but I speak concerning Christ and the church. Nevertheless let each one of you in particular so love his own wife as himself. … (vv. 25–33)

It is interesting to note how much ink is given to husbands in comparison to wives. Of the twelve verses specifically directed to husbands and wives in Ephesians 5, only three are directed toward wives, while the remaining nine are primarily directed toward husbands. This underscores my point that husbands are the ones who should be taking the lead in their marriages. Then what is God primarily calling a husband to do? It can be summed up in three words: love your wife. I firmly believe that it is husbands who hold the key to a flourishing marriage, because they are the initiators. A wife will come into full fruition and submission in response to her husband loving her as he should: as Christ loved the church. If this sounds like a tall order, you're absolutely right. It is. But that is the example we are given to follow: to love as Christ loved the church.

How did Jesus Christ initially demonstrate His love toward us? It was through His death. In John 15:13, Jesus said, "'Greater love has no one than this, than to lay down one's life for his friends.'" Then in Romans 5:8 we read, "God demonstrates His own love toward us, in that while we were still sinners, Christ died for us." We were once in rebellion against God, and our hearts were hardened against Him. But one day, we came into a realization of what Jesus did for us. Our hearts softened, and we responded and put our faith in Him. The Bible tells us, "We love Him because He first loved us" (1 John 4:19). So our love for Christ is a direct response to His persistent and patient love for us.

In the same way, a wife's respect of her husband and willingness to follow his leadership is rooted in his loving her as Christ loved the church. Just as the church has responded to Christ because of His overwhelming love, so will a wife respond to her husband for the same reason.

Our goal as husbands should be to simply fulfill God's

command to us and leave her reaction up to Him. We should not love her so she will submit to us or follow us; we should love her because we are commanded to.

THE LEADERSHIP PARADOX

So how do we do that? Let's look at another passage:

> Let nothing be done through selfish ambition or conceit, but in lowliness of mind let each esteem others better than himself. Let each of you look out not only for his own interests, but also for the interests of others. Let this mind be in you which was also in Christ Jesus, who, being in the form of God, did not consider it robbery to be equal with God, but made Himself of no reputation, taking the form of a bondservant, and coming in the likeness of men. And being found in appearance as a man, He humbled Himself and became obedient to the point of death, even the death of the cross. (Phil. 2:3–8)

If we are going to love our wives as Christ loved the church, then we need to follow the pattern given here in Philippians 2, among other places. To love as Christ loves is to place my wife's needs ahead of my own and to esteem her needs above my needs. Remember, Jesus said, "For even the Son of Man did not come to be served, but to serve, and to give His life a ransom for many" (Mark 10:45). He came to serve. So husbands are to serve their wives. They are to love their wives. Remember, before a word is given regarding the submission of a wife to her husband, the Bible tells us to submit to one another in the fear of God (see Eph. 5:21).

Coming back to Philippians 2, we read in verse 7 that Jesus "made Himself of no reputation." Another way to translate this is, "He emptied himself." Did He empty himself of His divinity? Absolutely not. Never, at any time, did Jesus cease to be God. He never voided His deity, although you could say that He veiled it. Rather, He laid aside the privilege of deity when He walked among us as a man. Although He was God, although He could do anything that He wanted to, basically,

He allowed Himself to face the limitations of the human body. He was hungry. He was thirsty. He was weary. He felt sorrow. He went through the range of human emotions. He emptied Himself of the privileges of deity, walked among us as a man, and He was our servant. This was so dramatically illustrated in the upper room when Jesus laid aside His outer garment, got down on His hands and knees, and washed the feet of the disciples. Truly, He humbled himself.

You may be thinking, "Oh, I can't do that. If I were to humble myself like that my wife would walk all over me. She would take complete advantage of me." But that is not necessarily true. And even if it were, so what? Don't focus so much on her response. Rather do what God has called you to do. In other words, read your own mail! Don't lecture your wife on what the Bible says to her; take heed to what the Bible says to you as a man and as a husband. Here is something important to know about leadership. It is rooted in a paradox. The fact is, true authority comes from humility. It is not a matter of weakness, but of meekness. By meekness, I mean power under constraint. Your wife knows what you want to do; she knows what your desire is. But in loving her as Christ loves the church, you must be willing to surrender that.

So what does that mean in practical terms for us as husbands? Well, in my house, for starters, it means letting my wife have the remote control. This is very hard for me, because I love to dominate it. I am Mr. Channel Surfer. Usually I will start clicking when a commercial comes on, because I hate commercials. I will surf along and watch a little bit of a program, maybe three minutes, and then go over to something else. I'll watch that for twelve seconds, then something else for ten minutes. Cathe will start getting into a program, and then a commercial comes on. Click. I've moved on to something else. It drives her crazy. So for me to turn that control over to her is the ultimate expression of dying to myself. For you, dying to yourself and putting your wife's needs above your own might mean something else.

I know it's hard to give up that control, but as I said, spiritual authority is rooted in paradox. Jesus said, "But whoever desires to become great among you shall be your servant. And whoever of you desires to be first shall be slave of all" (Mark 10:43–44). Authority does not mean that you manipulate your wife or lord over her. That is tyrannical. In fact, a husband who constantly lectures his wife on his authority probably has very little. That is not to say that a man shouldn't be firm and decisive and show leadership ability. But it does mean that he is to be humble and unselfish. It means that he is to rule with humility. It is what God asks of us: "He has shown you, *O man*, what is good; and what does the Lord require of you but to do justly, to love mercy, and to walk humbly with your God?" (Micah 6:8, emphasis mine).

Now I know this flies in the face of the stereotypical, macho-man concept of the tough guy who asserts himself, always is in control, and whose wife comes at his beck and call. But that is not God's way. Nor is it loving our wives as God has called us to. That is not the way we are to lead as husbands, because it takes more for a man to humble himself than to assert himself. What it takes is true love. And God requires nothing less than just that.

IT'S HOW YOU DEFINE IT

But what does love mean, really? Sometimes it is hard to define, because in our English language, we basically have one word for "love." We use it to describe everything from "I love my dog" to "I love golf" to "I love my wife." Yet in Greek, the original language of the New Testament, there are many words for "love." There is *erōs*, which primarily refers to love on the physical plane. This is where our English word, "erotic," comes from. There is *philĕō*, which is love on the emotional plane. Our English word, "Philadelphia," meaning, "house of brotherly love," is derived from *philĕō*. There is *storgē*, which refers to family love, as in the love for parents or children. Then, there is *agapē*, which speaks of a sacrificial, spiritual love. This word, by the way, is the word that is used most frequently in the New Testament when you read the word, "love." It is also the word used in Ephesians 5:25: "Husbands, love [*agapē*] your wives. ... " In other words, love her with that sacrificial, all-giving love.

This is not to say that *erōs*, and even *philĕō*, do not have a part to play in a marriage. When you first saw your wife, you most likely found her physically attractive. So *erōs* does play a part. Yet we tend to equate the word, "erotic," with evil, because it is usually presented in a twisted and perverted manner. But *erōs* is a God-given love, and in its proper place, it can be blessed by the Lord. Of course, that proper place is within the parameters and safety of the marriage relationship. The sexual union between a husband and wife is a way to express their intimacy, their oneness with each other, and of course, for the purpose of bearing children. But it is something that God designed uniquely for a man and a woman who are committed in marriage to enjoy. The problem with *erōs* is that it is essentially selfish. *Erōs* basically says, "I want something from you. Give it to me now." While *erōs* has its place in marriage, you can't build a marriage on it.

Then there is *philĕō*. In many ways, *philĕō* is a love that is nobler than *erōs*, because it is a give-and-take love. It is really a love that says, "I love you if you love me," or "I love you as long as I find something lovable in you." It is a love that expects something back. *Philĕō* is a love that springs from the sense of pleasure we draw from the object or the person loved. You feel good when you are with that person. He or she is fun to be with, makes you laugh, or entertains you. You love that person because of what he or she brings to the relationship, and you are loved for the same reason.

This world's love is primarily object-oriented. A person is loved because of his or her physical attractiveness, personality, wit, prestige, talent, or some other feature or trait that we happen to find appealing. We love someone because they made it into *People* magazine's "50 Most Beautiful People" issue. Or, we love the way they sing. We love the way they write. We love the way they do this or that. The problem is that this is a fickle kind of love. If that trait that we find lovable—like beauty, for example—is diminished by age, or someone more talented or gifted comes along, then this fickle love is transferred.

Here is the problem: many people enter into marriage with nothing more than *erōs* and *philĕō*. "I want this from you." "I love you as long as you are attractive to me, appealing to me, and I find what I want from you. But the moment you cease to do that for me, I am going to move on. I don't want you in my life anymore." Then the marriage is dissolved because of "irreconcilable differences."

In contrast to *erōs* and *philĕō*, *agapē* springs from a sense of preciousness of the object being loved. *Agapē* is primarily determined by the character of the one who loves and not necessarily whether the object is necessarily lovable. *Agapē* is not a mere feeling or emotion. It is far more. This is the kind of love God commands us to have as husbands.

God commands us as husbands to love our wives with *agapē*—not with this fickle love that merely loves if she lovable. *Agapē* loves in spite of all of that. Yet this love transforms the one who is being loved. As you love your wife like this, it will change her, just as Christ loved you like this and it changed you.

The husband who loves his wife for what she can give him loves as the world loves, and not as Christ loves. But the husband who loves his wife as Christ loves the church gives everything he has for his wife, including his own life, if necessary. If a loving husband is willing to sacrifice his own life, then how much more should he be willing to make lesser sacrifices for her, such as his own likes and dislikes, desires, opinions, preferences, and personal welfare? How much more should he be willing to set these aside to please her and meet her needs? He dies to self in order to live for his wife, because this is what Christ's love demands.

So really instead of lecturing your wife on what she is supposed to do, why don't you look at what you are supposed to do? Make sure you are loving your wife as Christ loved the church.

HELP OR HINDRANCE?

In addition to loving our wives as Christ loved the church, we are told in Ephesians 5: "Husbands, love your wives, just as Christ also loved the church and gave Himself for her, that He might sanctify and cleanse her with the washing of water by the word … " (vv. 25–26). No one can be a greater hindrance to a wife's spiritual growth than her husband, but on the other hand, no one can be a greater encouragement. A husband's first priority is to make sure his wife is properly aligned with God. He recognizes that her personal happiness as a woman, a wife, and a mother all hinge on that. Some husbands might say, "That's not my problem. That's her problem." But that is not the case, because God has called husbands to lead spiritually. The husband is to be the spiritual leader in the home, as 1 Peter 3:7 tells us, "Husbands, likewise, dwell with them with understanding, giving honor to the wife, as to the weaker vessel, and as being heirs together of the grace of life, that your prayers may not be hindered."

We might look at 1 Peter 3:7 and say, "I think I have that part down: 'Dwell with your wife. …' I do dwell with her. So I'm doing all right there." But that phrase, "dwell with," means, "Be aligned. Be one in thoughts, goals, and aspirations." This comes back to the original concept that God gave us in Genesis and that is spoken of in Ephesians 5: " 'For this reason a man shall leave his father and mother and be joined to his wife, and the two shall become one flesh' " (v. 31). Leave and cleave—remember, those are two operative words in a successful marriage. You leave all other relationships and cleave to your wife, realizing that she should be your best friend in life. You are aligned to her, dwelling with her.

If you fail to do this as a husband, Scripture warns that your prayers will be hindered. Your prayer life will be hindered if your house is out of order, that is, if you are not dwelling with your wife as you ought to. This is the same principle Jesus was speaking of when He said, "Therefore if you bring your gift to the altar, and there remember that your brother has something against you, leave your gift there before the altar, and go your way. First be reconciled to your brother, and then come and offer your gift" (Matt. 5:23–24). This is speaking of prayer. If you are coming before the throne of God in prayer, and you know that someone has something against you or is angry with you, first try to resolve it. If you don't, it can hinder your prayer life. In the same way, if your house is out of order, if you are neglecting your responsibilities as a spiritual leader to your wife and children, then it can hinder your prayer life. We must take care of our home and lead. Our priorities should be God first, then family, and then our occupations or ministries.

I know this is hard to do. It isn't any easier for me than it is for any other man. I have to consistently ask myself, am I loving my wife as Christ loves the church? Am I laying my life down? Am I being the leader God has called me to be? It is a constant process of realignment and fine-tuning, because we can be doing great as husbands and fathers one day and fall short the next.

ASK FOR HELP

You might be thinking today, "But Greg, you say the primary responsibility is with the husband and the responsibility rests on his shoulders. How can I do it? I can't." I can't either, because this doesn't come naturally for me. I am not naturally wired this way. No one is. So what do we do? Remember, in our last chapter we talked about the importance of being filled with the Spirit. Before a word is said in Ephesians 5 about mutual submission or about wives submitting to their husbands or about husbands loving their wives as Christ loved the church, we are told, "Be filled with the Spirit" (v. 17). We can't do it on our own. We need supernatural help.

This love that God is commanding us to have for our wives is something that comes from Him. Romans 5:5 says, "Now hope does not disappoint, because the love of God has been poured out in our hearts by the Holy Spirit who was given to us." We must ask God to work this love into our lives. It will come as a result of walking closely with Him, because "the fruit of the Spirit is love … " (Gal. 5:22).

You won't get there overnight. It will take a lifetime. But determine to move in that direction today and say, "I am going to be the man that God has called me to be. From this day forward, I am going to seek to love my wife as Christ loved the church."

STRENGTH TRAINING

- *Think of one area in which you could begin setting aside your own needs and giving priority to your wife's needs. Step out in faith and start today, asking God to help you and empower you through the Holy Spirit.*

DAILY SUPPLEMENTS

- *Each day this week, read one of the following selections from* Marriage Connections: *"In and Under Authority," "Just Love Her," "As Christ Loved the Church," "Sacrificial Love," "Purifying Love," "Dwell with Understanding," and "Submission Is a Two-Way Street."*

Nevertheless let each one of you in particular so love his own wife as himself, and let the wife see that she respects her husband. (Ephesians 5:33)

WHAT GOD SAYS TO WIVES

When Mattel first introduced Teen Talk Barbie some years ago, one among many of the statements she made triggered a great public outcry. Three little words generated such a public relations dilemma for Mattel that Teen Talk Barbie had to be yanked from the market until she changed her tune. The offending remark? "Math is hard." Perhaps if Ken had said the same thing, no one would have even noticed. But as this Barbie inadvertently confirmed, there is a hypersensitivity in our culture regarding what a woman is—or is not.

If ever there were a concept relating to women that was unpopular today, it would be the one we're about to look at in Scripture. Many would say the concepts found there are outdated and archaic in our now-liberated society. Yes, they are old-fashioned to some, but to others, they are on the cutting edge. More importantly, they work, quite simply, because they are true. They are God's order for a woman and a wife. As we look at the state of the American family, we can safely say the reason it is falling apart is because we have strayed from God's standards.

As I pointed out in the previous chapter, I firmly believe the breakdown of the family can, to a great degree, be laid at the feet of men today, because the role of the man in the home is that of initiator and leader. Because men have largely failed to fulfill this responsibility God has given them, we see the effects in the home. A lot of women would nod in agreement, saying, "Yes, that's true. It's the failure of the men." But marriage is a two-way street. While men have their part in the relationship, which God has clearly laid out in Scripture, God also calls the woman to, among other things, submit to her husband as unto the Lord. "Wait a second," some wives are saying. "The Bible says, 'Husbands, love your wives, just as Christ also loved the church.' If my husband isn't loving me as Christ loved the church, then I must not be obligated to submit to him. After all, if he is the initiator, if he is the one who should be taking the lead and is failing to do that, then I am not under any responsibility to do my part." But the case before us in 1 Peter 3 contradicts that thinking:

> Wives, likewise, be submissive to your own husbands, that even if some do not obey the word, they, without a word, may be won by the conduct of their wives, when they observe your chaste conduct accompanied by fear. Do not let your adornment be merely outward—arranging the hair, wearing gold, or putting on fine apparel—rather let it be the hidden person of the heart, with the incorruptible beauty of a gentle and quiet spirit, which is very precious in the sight of God. For in this manner, in former times, the holy women who trusted in God also adorned themselves, being submissive to their own husbands, as Sarah obeyed Abraham, calling him lord, whose daughters you are if you do good and are not afraid with any terror. (vv. 1–6)

This passage deals with a Christian woman who is married to a non-Christian man and what she can do to reach her husband for Christ. I also believe we could apply these verses to a Christian woman who is married to a nominally Christian man or a man who may name the name of Christ, but is not a spiritual leader. God has given wives a clear strategy to follow in reaching their husbands and clearly lays out the role and responsibilities of the Christian wife in the marriage relationship. In fact, as a wife begins to apply the principles found here, she might even see her husband become a new-and-improved model.

SILENT PREACHING

The strategy for reaching your husband, Peter says, is without a word. Here is a man who is an unbeliever, and his wife wants him to come to faith. She might think, "Maybe I should just hit him with a sermon every single day. When he comes home from work, I will preach to him. I will make him watch Christian TV programs with me. I will do whatever I can." Though there is a place for preaching and the like, there is also a place for living it. What you need to do is let God reach him by the Holy Spirit, and you need to live the life. It is not merely preaching to him, but it is also backing up that preaching with a godly life.

This may describe your situation. You may be married to an unbeliever, which unfortunately happens quite often. Sometimes it happens because a man and a woman get married, and then the woman comes to faith in Christ. But sadly, and more often than we would like to admit, there are Christian women who just get impatient with waiting on God and go out and marry some man who is not a follower of Jesus Christ. Somehow they think the verse that says, "Do not be unequally yoked together with unbelievers" (2 Cor. 6: 14) doesn't apply to them. But then some time passes, and they are miserable in that relationship. I have even had some of these women over the years come to me and say, "I have met this really great Christian guy at church. God has told me that I can divorce my non-Christian husband and marry this Christian guy." I have heard it the other way around too. Christian guys have come to me and said, "God has told me that I can divorce my non-Christian wife and marry this Christian woman."

But I can guarantee that God didn't tell them this, because 1 Corinthians 7:13 says, "And a woman who has a husband who does not believe, if he is willing to live with her, let her not divorce him." That sounds pretty clear to me. We also read in 1 Corinthians 7:27, "Are you bound to a wife? Do not seek to be loosed. Are you loosed from a wife? Do not seek a wife." So believers who are married to unbelievers should stick with that commitment and pray that the unbelieving spouse will come to his or her senses and come to the Lord. It will happen by showing, as opposed to preaching alone. Live a godly life, and God will do the saving.

INSPIRATION OR MANIPULATION?

Telling a woman that the way to reach her husband is by not saying anything is one of the most difficult things you could ask. Women, by nature, are very verbal. They have the ability to persuade. Now, this is a God-given ability, but it all depends for what and to whom it is yielded. If this gift is yielded for good to God, it can have a profound influence. But if it is yielded for evil to Satan, it can be destructive.

For example, consider how Esther was able to use her feminine influence to spare a generation of Jewish people. Then look at how Eve misused her feminine influence to move her husband in the wrong direction. Of course, Adam was responsible for what he did, but she helped facilitate the process. You see, what wives must avoid is manipulation, that is, trying to do things that would move her husband to do what she wants to do. Manipulation can be defined as "managing or influencing by artful or devious skill."

Wives must avoid this temptation to manipulate, because it will never bring about lasting change. I know it's tempting when he doesn't seem to be listening. You want to help out God a little bit, so you think, "I'll just weld the knob on his radio to a Christian station and then crank the volume all the way up. ..." "I'll put little gospel tracts in his sandwiches. Instead of turkey, it will be *The Four Spiritual Laws*. ..." "I will just get Christian guys to seek him out and try to talk to him." He can tell what you are trying to do. He can see what is going on. And most likely, he will rebel from it. It will drive him away instead of drawing him in. Attempting to nag him into the kingdom will not have the effect you were hoping for.

Solomon, who had many, many wives and knew a little bit about nagging, had this to say in Proverbs 19:13: "A nagging wife annoys like a constant dripping" (NLT). Well put, Solomon. It's like a faucet that keeps dripping and dripping, nonstop. Another observation from Solomon, recorded in Proverbs 21:19, says, "Better to dwell in the wilderness, than with a contentious and angry woman." Women nag when their husbands don't seem to be paying attention to them, so they keep pressing the point until hopefully he gets the message. But the fact of the matter is that nagging doesn't reach a man. Actually, it drives him away.

It is very easy to only pick up on the negatives. "You didn't take out the trash. Why don't you clean the toothpaste off the mirror? You didn't wash your whiskers down the sink. You left your tools out when you were working on the car. When are you going to fix this?" Does all he hear about is what is wrong? He also needs to hear about what is right. He needs to hear that you appreciate him … that you love him … that you find him attractive. Wives, please know that your husbands need to hear this. Don't assume that men are so self-assured that they don't need to hear these things. They do. They need to be stroked a little bit. Maybe a lot. They need to be encouraged. They need to be reassured.

While I do not condone this whatsoever, I want to point out that one reason a man often gets involved with another woman is because someone will come along and pay attention to him and tell him he is so wonderful and so special. Then he goes home and perhaps never hears that from his wife. He even wonders at times if his wife still loves him. Wives need to verbally communicate that to their husbands.

But the primary concept of the idea of winning your husband without a word is what could be described as "the silent preaching of a lovely life." It is to first prepare the ground of his heart by living out your faith in the home. If you fail to do this, he will never listen to your message and will actually have an excuse for his unbelief. But on the other hand, if you break up the soil of his heart with your actions, your words will have far greater impact and will eventually take root.

This same principle could be applied to other people in our lives, whether it is parents, children, friends, or coworkers whom we are praying will come to faith in Christ. They don't need a sermon every day. They have heard your message. Now live it. Show yourself to be a Christian in practical, tangible ways, and that will open their hearts to the seed of the Word of God. They will see a distinct difference in your lifestyle as a result of your knowing Jesus Christ. That will speak volumes to them. It was Augustine who once wrote, "Preach the gospel, and when necessary, use words."

Jesus told us that we are to be the salt of the earth and the light of the world (see Matt. 5:13–14). Many of us are light without being salt, and sometimes we are salt without being light. Being light without being salt means that we talk about our faith. We proclaim it. But we are not living it. Being salt means that we are having an effect on people around us, but perhaps we are not talking about our faith as much as we should. There is a place for both salt and light. There is a place for testimony and speaking for Christ and a place for living the life. Both go hand-in-hand. It's a powerful combination.

A wife must be willing to leave the work of conversion up to the Holy Spirit and seek to prepare the soil of her husband's heart by living a godly life through submission. This isn't taught exclusively in 1 Peter 3. We know that Ephesians 5 says,

> Wives, submit to your own husbands, as to the Lord. For the husband is head of the wife, as also Christ is head of the church; and He is the Savior of the body. Therefore, just as the church is subject to Christ, so let the wives be to their own husbands in everything. (vv. 22–24)

As I pointed out in Chapter 3, it is worth noting that before that infamous and often-quoted verse about wives submitting to their husbands is given, there is a verse that precedes it, which says, "Submitting to one another in the fear of God" (v. 21). What an insight that is. Submission is not merely taught to wives and women; it is taught to men and women, and specifically, husbands and wives. Before a word is said about the role of the wife or the role of the husband specifically, we are told to submit ourselves one to another in the fear of God. That is foundational. Put the needs of your spouse before your own.

MISCONCEPTIONS ABOUT SUBMISSION

What does it mean to submit? I covered this earlier. Originally, it was a military term meaning, "to arrange or rank yourself under." The principal idea of submission is that of relinquishing your rights to another person. When we apply this idea to marriage, it usually is the last thing we want to do. So many marriages are in trouble today, because one person enters into a marriage wanting to know what the other person can do for him or her. "How can you meet my needs? How can you make my life easier? How can you fulfill me?" Because people are seeking to find fulfillment in marriage, their marriages are falling apart. They have unrealistic expectations.

One word of advice I have often shared with those who are single is not to get married in an attempt to find fulfillment. We should find our ultimate fulfillment in a relationship with Jesus Christ and be content where we are. The apostle Paul said, "For I have learned in whatever state I am, to be content" (Phil. 4:11). Yet so many people go into marriage thinking, "What can you do for me? How can you meet my needs?" The great barriers to successful marriages are self and selfishness.

However, there are limits to submission. Do you what your husband says, no matter what? No. The Scripture teaches in Colossians 3:18, "Wives, submit to your own husbands, as is fitting in the Lord." For instance, let's say your husband asks you to do something that is unscriptural. You are not bound to that. Nor does submission mean that you would allow him to physically abuse you. Some wives have been told by overbearing husbands, "You must submit to whatever I dish out." But that is wrong. God has not called you to be abused or to place yourself or your children in a place of physical danger. That is not what God's Word means when it speaks of submission.

Yet there is a place of submission in the marriage relationship that God has given to the wife. Ephesians 5:22 says that wives are to submit to their husbands "as to the Lord." Colossians 3:17 says, "And whatever you do in word or deed, *do all in the name of the Lord Jesus*" (emphasis mine). A few verses later we read, "And whatever you do, do it heartily, as to the Lord and not to men" (Colossians 3:23). The key to submission to your husband is to do it as unto the Lord. Do it as though Jesus himself had asked it of you. Do it as an act of worship to God, and that can change the whole picture. Suddenly, it is something you are doing for the Lord, not just for your husband.

For a wife to submit to her husband does not mean that she is less important than he is. According to Galatians 3:28, "There is neither Jew nor Greek, there is neither slave nor free, there is neither male nor female; for you are all one in Christ Jesus." A man doesn't have greater access to God than a woman does, nor does a woman have greater access to God than a man does. Although a husband and wife are different in some ways, they have equal access before the Lord.

Even so, we must recognize the distinctions and differences between men and women. To blur these lines and to pretend they don't exist isn't wise. Instead of failing to recognize these differences, we should be celebrating them. It is not an issue of superiority or inferiority. It is simply a matter of recognizing the specific roles that husbands and wives both have to make a marriage all that God wants it to be.

So let your husband be the leader. Encourage him in that role, and even let him make a few mistakes in the process. He may not do it perfectly, but recognize it as a God-given responsibility that has been placed on his shoulders.

LOOKING GOOD

Returning to 1 Peter 3, we come to the subject of outward appearance:

> Do not let your adornment be merely outward—arranging the hair, wearing gold, or putting on fine apparel—rather let it be the hidden person of the heart, with the incor-

ruptible beauty of a gentle and quiet spirit, which is very precious in the sight of God. For in this manner, in former times, the holy women who trusted in God also adorned themselves, being submissive to their own husbands."

The word, "adorning," used here comes from the Greek word cosmos, from which we get the English word, "cosmetic." Peter is talking about majoring on the outside while ignoring the inside. As we look at this passage, it is necessary to understand the culture of the time. Roman women were given over to the latest fashion crazes. They were very focused on appearance. In fact, some of the engravings from this era indicate that women wore towering hairdos with nets of gold and expensive combs. They also would wear gold rings, necklaces, and bracelets around their necks, ankles, arms, and so forth. They would spend a great deal of time on the outward.

So Peter was saying not to flaunt this type of thing or make it your primary focus. The phrase, "putting on fine apparel," is not implying that it is wrong for a Christian woman to be fashion-conscious or attractive. But what this passage is saying is that it's wrong to make that her only focus. In fact, "putting on fine apparel" could be translated, "the frequent changing of clothing." It conveys the idea of a woman who is constantly changing her clothes for the purpose of impressing people. She wants everyone to notice how great she looks. Peter was saying, "Don't make this your focus in life. Think about the inner person. Think about the inside."

When it comes to this passage in Scripture, I'm sometimes asked, "What do you think about makeup? Should a woman wear makeup?" My answer to that is, to quote Charles Swindoll, "If a house needs painting, then paint it!" But be concerned with the inside of the house as well as the outside. Don't be concerned only with the outer facade, because the inside is what really matters. This is what is really being addressed here.

In the description of the virtuous wife in Proverbs 31, we are told she is aware of her outward appearance. She goes about her work with vigor and strengthens her arms. I don't know if she did arm curls or if they had Hebrew aerobics back then. But she is a woman who cares about the way she looks. A wife shouldn't neglect this. While some women go too far and seem to only think about how they appear, others go too far the other way and don't think about their appearance often enough.

We hear the verse, "For bodily exercise profits a little" (1 Tim. 4:8), which is often quoted by overweight or out-of-shape people. While it's true that bodily exercise profits a little, at least it does profit some. The remainder of the verse says, "But godliness is profitable for all things, having promise of the life that now is and of that which is to come." Think of it as temple maintenance. Your body is the temple of the Holy Spirit, and you should do what you can as a Christian woman to continue to be outwardly attractive to your husband. Even so, you should not do it at the expense of being inwardly beautiful.

Inner beauty is a very appealing quality that a Christian woman develops over the years. It is not a beauty that is achieved with makeup or with clothes alone. Rather, it is a glow that comes from the inside. It is such a wonderful quality. This is what 1 Peter 3:4 is speaking of: "Let it be the hidden person of the heart, with the incorruptible beauty of a gentle and quiet spirit, which is very precious in the sight of God." Or as another translation puts it, "The unfading loveliness of a calm and gentle spirit" (PHILLIPS).

Referring to "the hidden person of the heart," this phrase does not mean that a wife must sit around in silence and cannot disagree with her husband or offer a different opinion. She should speak her mind and try to influence her husband for good. I would even venture to say that she has a God-given right and responsibility to set her husband straight if he is off course. I have come to respect my wife Cathe's opinions over the years. She has a way of seeing through a situation. I find that she often has discernment and observations about people that I might otherwise miss or overlook. She provides insight and wisdom, and that is virtue.

LOVE HIM, BUT LIKE HIM TOO

Finally, I want to point out that when the Scripture says that wives are to love their husbands, the word used for "love" in the original language is the Greek word, *phileō*. As I mentioned in the previous chapter, this is one of several words for love in the Greek language. It refers to a friendship love. It is a given that wives should *agapē* their husbands, which is a sacrificial, spiritual love. Yet wives are to *phileō* their husbands as well. Loosely translated, "Wives, like your husbands." Don't just love him. Like him, and let him know. Reassure him. He needs to hear that from you. And, let him lead—even if he doesn't do it perfectly. Let him make a few mistakes, but strengthen him in that leadership role. Don't undermine it. Don't try to make it difficult for him. Instead, make it easier. It is a lot of responsibility to bear, and it is not as easy as you may think. Your husband needs your prayers. He needs your support. He needs your encouragement. He needs to be reaffirmed of your commitment to him and of your love for him.

So wives, submit to your husbands as to the Lord and win him without a word. Concentrate on the inner. How true it is when Scripture says, "Charm is deceitful and beauty is passing, but a woman who fears the Lord, she shall be praised" (Proverbs 31:30). Concentrate on the responsibilities God has given to you, and by the power of His Spirit, He will help you to be the woman He wants you to be.

If you are a husband reading this today and have, by God's grace, found yourself married to such a woman, don't take it for granted. Proverbs 18:22 says, "He who finds a wife finds a good thing, and obtains favor from the Lord." If you have found a godly woman that is dedicated to Jesus Christ and has made a commitment to you, then you have a treasure of greater value than everything else.

STRENGTH TRAINING

- *Have you struggled with the idea of submitting to your husband? Ask God to begin revealing to you those areas in which you have been resisting your husband's leadership. Then turn them over to the Lord, asking Him to help you be the wife He is calling you to be.*

- *Are you married to an unbelieving husband? Pray for God's wisdom in how you can demonstrate, in practical ways, His love for your husband. Also, ask a godly woman whom you can confide in to pray regularly for you.*

DAILY SUPPLEMENTS

- *Each day this week, read one of the following selections from* Marriage Connections: *"The Motive and Manner of Submission," "The Model of Submission," "The Limits to Submission," "Without a Word," "Inward and Outer Beauty," "A Remarkable Letter," and "Honor God in All Things."*

Death and life are in the power of the tongue,
and those who love it will eat its fruit.
(Proverbs 18:21)

THE INCREDIBLE POWER OF WORDS

A few years ago, Cathe and I were invited to stay at a cabin in Virginia that belonged to some friends. This cabin didn't have any heat to speak of, except for a fireplace and a little furnace downstairs that had to be fed a regular diet of logs. I told the owners, "I know this might sound stupid, but I don't know how to build a fire very well."

They said, "You have to go out and get some kindling."

"OK. Where do you buy that?"

"You don't buy it," they told me. "You go find it. Kindling is the little branches and things that you use to start the fire."

Then they showed me the proper way to start a fire, and pointed out that once the fireplace is filled with enough ash, I would need to scoop it out, put it into a metal bucket, and then keep the bucket on a concrete surface so all of the embers will cool down.

"Be careful to make sure they have all cooled down," they cautioned. "They do stay quite live for a period of time."

It was freezing cold outside, so we had the fireplace and furnace going nonstop. I would get up at 3:00 a.m. to add more wood to the fires. After awhile, the fireplace was filled with ashes. I got out the shovel and filled the bucket all the way to the brim. I waited for what I thought had been a couple of days, then decided it was time to empty the bucket. It was late at night, and Cathe was already asleep. I went outside in my PJs and slippers, took this bucket of ash, and pitched it out into the forest. As I did, everything seemed to move in slow motion. Much to my horror, I saw, in the ash, these little burning embers. Immediately, small fires were starting—three fires right off the bat. I started picking up the live, burning embers with my hands and throwing them up on the driveway. Then a breeze came along and more little fires erupted. I ran into the cabin to look for some kind of bucket and found one that looked slightly larger than a drinking glass. So I filled it with water, poured it on the fire, and ran back again. You'd better believe that I was calling on the Lord for help. I thought I would burn the whole forest down, but fortunately, that didn't happen. The rest of the night, I kept looking out, thinking I would see a huge forest fire.

That experience reminded me of the truth of the statement James made when he said, "So also, the tongue is a small thing, but what enormous damage it can do. A tiny spark can set a great forest on fire" (James 3:5 NLT). How true that is. More people have died by the power of the tongue than by any other weapon humanity has ever devised. We have seen the massive destruction that came as a result of nuclear weapons on Nagasaki and Hiroshima. We have seen what happens when strict safety standards are not followed, such as the disaster at Chernobyl.

THE WORLD'S MOST DANGEROUS WEAPON

Today, manufacturers place warning labels on their products so that we won't do something stupid. They are trying to protect themselves from potential lawsuits. Consider all of the safety standards we have in place for everything from automobile emissions to gun control. Yet the most dangerous weapon and the most toxic pollutant is left unchecked: the tongue.

We desperately need to learn how to control it, and especially in our marriages. If we were brutally honest, I am sure we could look back on this past year (or maybe even the past week) and admit we have said a few things to our spouse that we have lived to regret. Dedicated to God, our tongues can be a powerful force for good in our marriages and in the lives of those around us. But left unchecked, especially when yielded to the enemy, the tongue is the most destructive weapon on the face of the earth. It can tear down marriages and destroy lives.

As followers of Jesus Christ, we know a lot about certain sins we should avoid. We know that we aren't supposed to lie. We know that we aren't supposed to steal. We know that we aren't supposed to be immoral. We go out of our way to avoid things that would drag us down spiritually. Yet one thing we are warned about many times in Scripture is often left unchecked among believers. It is also an area that is grossly neglected by many husbands and wives, and that is thinking about what we say.

For example, we would never dream of taking out a knife and thrusting it into our husband or wife. Yet we can wound our partner deeply with a few carelessly spoken words. It is a very real problem and we would do well as husbands and wives to learn how to bring this area under control. The Book of James offers some wise observations about the tongue:

> We all stumble in many ways. If anyone is never at fault in what he says, he is a perfect man, able to keep his whole body in check.

> When we put bits into the mouths of horses to make them obey us, we can turn the whole animal. Or take ships as an example. Although they are so large and are driven by strong winds, they are steered by a very small rudder wherever the pilot wants to go. Likewise the tongue is a small part of the body, but it makes great boasts. Consider what a great forest is set on fire by a small spark. The tongue also is a fire, a world of evil among the parts of the body. It corrupts the whole person, sets the whole course of his life on fire, and is itself set on fire by hell.

> All kinds of animals, birds, reptiles and creatures of the sea are being tamed and have been tamed by man, but no man can tame the tongue. It is a restless evil, full of deadly poison.

> With the tongue we praise our Lord and Father, and with

it we curse men, who have been made in God's likeness. Out of the same mouth come praise and cursing. My brothers, this should not be. (James 3:2–10 NIV)

James tells us that the tongue is like a fire, like a bit, like a beast, and like a poison, among other things.

Take James' example of the bit. We can make a large horse turn around and go wherever we want by means of a small bit in its mouth. A few years ago at the Rose Parade, I watched a man riding a buffalo down the street. He had a saddle on it and a bit in its mouth. It was amazing to me that this rider could control a massive beast with a tiny bit. Just as a bit controls a horse (or a buffalo in some cases), we are controlled by our words. One word can set the course that your life takes. Saying "I do" to a partner in marriage means a lifetime of commitment. Saying "I won't" to the temptation of an extramarital affair could save that marriage from destruction. Of course, saying "I will" to Jesus Christ will forever change your eternal destiny. Our tongues control us. What we say affects what we do. It also profoundly affects our marriages.

The tongue is a small thing, but what an enormous amount of damage it can do. This mere, two ounces of mucus membrane in our mouths can do so much evil or so much good. Think of those who have dedicated their words to darkness and to the devil. There was Adolf Hitler, for example, who, through his demonic rhetoric, led an entire nation down the pathway to hell and it resulted in the useless and needless slaughter of so many people. This is what a tongue dedicated to the devil can do.

Then we have the example of someone who has dedicated his words to God: Billy Graham. The result has been millions of people who have given their lives to Jesus Christ.

So to whom—and to what—are you dedicating your words? Are you dedicating them to God, and toward the goal of building up your husband, your family, and other people God has placed in your life?

TAKE TIME TO LISTEN

James 1:19 is a verse I think we should post where we can see it on a daily basis: "My dear brothers and sisters, be quick to listen, slow to speak, and slow to get angry … " (NLT). The problem is that too often we are swift to speak, slow to listen, and quick to get angry. But James is saying, "Be quick to listen." In other words, take the time to hear something out. Have you ever made a statement to your spouse or your children based on an incorrect understanding of what was happening, because you didn't take the time to hear them out? You were quick to make a snap judgment. That is why the Bible says, "What a shame, what folly, to give advice before listening to the facts!" (Prov. 18:13 NLT). I think that in our time of instant messaging and ten-second sound bites, we find it hard to slow down, be still, and listen. But we need to be quick to listen—and we need to be especially quick to hear what our husband or wife has to say.

One thing that I like to do is to communicate with Cathe throughout my day. I will call her up, tell her what's going on, and bring her up to speed. When I'm on a trip, I will call her and tell her about some experiences that I've had, and I am amazed at how much she remembers. Later, we'll be visiting with someone, and she will start telling a story that I told her. As she describes it, it is so vivid and accurate, I think, "Was she there with me?" After thirty-two years of marriage, she knows what I mean when I say certain words. She discerns things by the tone of my voice. Cathe is "quick to hear," and that is vitally important in a marriage.

A FAILURE TO COMMUNICATE

But often there is a breakdown in communication, and this begins to hurt the marriage. One husband was overheard saying to his wife, "Honey, what do you mean we don't communicate? Just yesterday. I e-mailed you a reply to the message you left on my voice mail!" That's twenty-first-century communication for you.

Still, it's amazing how a husband and wife who are trying

to communicate can talk past each other. What a wife says may translate into something entirely different for her husband. Likewise, what he says may mean something else to his wife. When a couple is driving somewhere and they get lost, she will say, "Let's ask for directions." But he hears, "You're not a man."

When she says, "Can I have the remote control?", he hears, "Let's watch something that will bore you beyond belief!"

She tells him, "You need to get in touch with your feelings."

He hears, "Blah, blah, blah."

She asks, "Are you listening to me?"

He hears, "Blah, blah, blah, blah, blah."

She says, "I would like to redecorate."

He hears, "Let's take our money and flush it down the toilet." What we have here is a failure to communicate. But we have to keep trying, don't we?

Not only should we be quick to listen, James tells us, but we also should be slow to get angry. As Proverbs 29:11 tells us, "A fool gives full vent to anger, but a wise person quietly holds it back" (NLT). Don't let anger control your life. Don't let it have a place in your marriage.

I heard about a husband and wife who, as newlyweds, decided to put into practice Ephesians 4:26, which says, " 'Be angry, and do not sin': do not let the sun go down on your wrath." So they determined never to go to bed mad at each other. Thirty years later, someone asked the husband how it worked out. He said, "Pretty well, but sometimes it was a little rough sitting up all night."

Yet there are certain people who are always mad about something. They never seem to be happy unless they are mad. They get over one thing and move on to another. They are always griping or complaining about something. The problem is, people who are often angry become bitter people. Bitter people rarely keep it to themselves—they want to spread it around. If you or your spouse fit this description, beware. It will infect your marriage and can also spread to your children and to others in your life. The Bible warns about a root of bitterness that can spring up and defile many (see Heb.

12:15). Don't let bitterness overtake your marriage.

Have you been wronged? Has someone hurt you? Has someone said something unkind about you? Perhaps it was your spouse. You need to forgive him or her. "But they don't deserve it," you say. Regardless of what someone has said or done to us, the Bible tells us, "And be kind to one another, tenderhearted, forgiving one another, even as God in Christ forgave you" (Eph. 4:32). You should extend forgiveness because God has extended forgiveness to you. When you forgive someone, you set a prisoner free: yourself. When you harbor bitterness, you are hurting yourself. You are hurting other people. You aren't helping anything. Let it go. Forgive. Put it behind you. Don't carry it any further.

QUIET, PLEASE

In addition to being slow to get angry, we should be slow to speak, which is really the thrust of what James is saying in these verses. A major part of self-control is mouth control. It is difficult to put your foot in your mouth when it's closed. That is something to think about. If we just would be quick to listen and slow to speak, we would avoid so much unnecessary misery. The Bible teaches that one day we will be held accountable for what we have said. Jesus said, "But I say to you that for every idle word men may speak, they will give account of it in the day of judgment. For by your words you will be justified, and by your words you will be condemned." (Matt. 12:36–37).

We speak a lot of words. It has been estimated that people speak enough words in one week to fill a 500-page book. But a true test of your faith is not the ability to speak your mind, but to hold your tongue. James is saying that if you want to be a spiritually mature person, you'll do it by learning to control your words. That is why the psalmist said, "I will watch what I do and not sin in what I say. I will curb my tongue when the ungodly are around me" (Psalm 39:1 NLT). We need to think about what we say, because there are many ways we can misuse our words.

Here is something to THINK about when you are talking

to your husband, wife, or anyone for that matter. When you are in doubt about something you are about to say, then apply this test:

T   Is it true?
H   Is it helpful?
I   Is it inspiring?
N   Is it necessary?
K   Is it kind?

You might be saying, "Give me a break! If I applied these standards, then 90 percent of what I said would not be said." So be it. Understand, even godly men and women struggle with keeping this area under control. Some of the greatest people that God ever used struggled with it. So don't feel like you're the only one.

Take Job, for instance. God himself said that Job was "blameless and upright" (see Job 1:8). Yet even Job had trouble controlling his own tongue. He said, "I am nothing—how could I ever find the answers? I will put my hand over my mouth in silence. I have said too much already. " (Job 40:4 NLT).

Isaiah was one of God's choice servants, but when he came into God's presence, the first things he became aware of were his words and how he used his tongue. He said, "Woe is me, for I am undone! Because I am a man of unclean lips, and I dwell in the midst of a people of unclean lips; for my eyes have seen the King, the Lord of hosts" (Isa. 6:5). When Isaiah was in the presence of God, he immediately became aware of the fact that he had misused his words and misused his tongue.

USE THEM WISELY

We have learned how not to use our words and our tongue. So how should we use them?

We should use them to glorify God. This is the highest and greatest use of our tongue because we were created to glorify God and give Him pleasure. James 3:9 says, "With [the tongue] we bless our God and Father, and with it we curse men, who have been made in the similitude of God."

It is important to remember that we were put on this earth to bring honor and praise to the One who created us. One of the ways we can do that is by what we say. Scripture is filled with numerous examples of verbal praise to God. David wrote, "Because Your lovingkindness is better than life, my lips shall praise You. Thus I will bless You while I live; I will lift up my hands in Your name" (Ps. 63:3–4). Ephesians 5:18–19 tells us, "Let the Holy Spirit fill and control you. Then you will sing psalms and hymns and spiritual songs among yourselves, making music to the Lord in your hearts" (NLT). Hebrews 13:15 says, "With Jesus' help, let us continually offer our sacrifice of praise to God by proclaiming the glory of his name" (NLT). God wants you to verbally glorify His name.

We should use them to build up one another—first and foremost, our husband or wife. The Bible says, "And let us not neglect our meeting together, as some people do, but encourage and warn each other, especially now that the day of his coming back again is drawing near" (Heb. 10:25 NLT). We need to encourage one another. We need to correct one another.

I believe the Lord wants us to reevaluate how we use our words with our spouse. Let's use them for the right reasons: to glorify God and to build up one another. Let's not use them for tearing down each other. Let's ask God to give us the strength in our marriages to use our words for His glory.

STRENGTH TRAINING

- *In what way does your husband or wife need to be genuinely encouraged today? Ask God to give you the right words to say.*
- *Have you recently hurt your spouse with your words? Ask for forgiveness.*

DAILY SUPPLEMENTS

- *Each day this week, read one of the following selections from* Marriage Connections: *"Pursuing Kindness," "A Second Honeymoon," "Radical Love," "Active Love," "Affirm Your Children," "Walk the Talk," and "Imitate God."*

God blesses the people who patiently endure testing. Afterward they will receive the crown of life that God has promised to those who love him.
(James 1:12 NLT)

STANDING STRONG AGAINST TEMPTATION

It seems as though everywhere you look, families are falling apart. It seems as though there is so little out there to strengthen and support the family today, and I think we could safely say, by and large, that Hollywood is no friend of the family.

The sad thing is that the television set is at the heart of so many of our homes. We let our children watch it unsupervised, which I think is highly inadvisable. Often it is going all day and all night in the background. Families once sat together at the table and talked at dinner, but now the television is usually blaring away. As one person put it, the new American hearth, the center for activities, conversation, and companionship is the television set.

Then there is the immorality constantly played out on our television screens and the big screen. We wonder why there is so much of this. Why are there so many programs that seem to attack the family and present other perverse versions of the family as viable alternatives? Is Hollywood creating the problem? Or is Hollywood merely reflecting the problem that already exists in our society? I think it's probably both. I think Hollywood adds to it and also reflects a very real problem in our culture and society, because clearly we are living in wicked times. These are the perilous days the Bible warns of (see 2 Tim. 3:1–9). These are the times of wickedness in the last days, where Satan has clearly set his sights on the church, on the family, and on believers.

We live in a culture today that is obsessed with sex—before marriage, outside of marriage, and in perverse forms. It just seems to get worse all the time. If historians were to look back at our time, they would have to conclude that this was a sex-obsessed culture. Of course, this should not surprise us, because Jesus said that in the last days, there would be wicked times, as it was in the days of Noah and in the days of Lot (see Luke 17:27–29). These both were times in human history uniquely characterized by sexual perversion.

FROM DECEPTION TO DEVASTATION

Of course, all of these things undermine marriages and families. Among them is adultery. It has spread throughout our society, and we see its effects all around. But how widespread is it? According to some statistics, 40 to 50 percent of all men have had extramarital affairs, and nearly 70 percent of all married men under 40 expect to have an extramarital relationship. But if you think this is a problem unique to men, think again. The women are catching up. Unfaithfulness on the part of women toward their husbands is now almost equal with that of the men.

Are you committing adultery? Are you planning to? Have you been thinking about it? Considering the statistics, it's entirely possible. I just want you to think for a few moments today about the repercussions and the damage this sin can bring to you, to your spouse, and to your family. It is something that is devastating in its impact. So significant is the sin of adultery that it made the top ten: the Ten Commandments, that is. "You shall not commit adultery," God says (Ex.20:14). Then God expands on it: "You shall not covet your neighbor's wife ... " (v. 17). Why did God give us commandments like these? It was for our own protection, because He knows what devastation it can bring.

The Bible asks the question, "Can a man take fire to his bosom, and his clothes not be burned?" (Prov. 6:27). The answer, of course, is no. As I pointed out in the last chapter, fire can get out of control so easily. That is how lust can be. You think, "I can contain this. I can handle this. This is no problem." Then suddenly the burning embers of lust are blowing over your life and you have lost all control. What happened? You took fire into your bosom, or into your heart or into your life, and you were burned. You were one of the many who thought you could handle it.

That is what Samson deluded himself into thinking. He thought, "What is this Delilah going to do to me? I am the mighty Samson. I can kill a thousand Philistines with the jawbone of a donkey. What is one little woman going to do to me?" But the devil was sly. He knew he could never bring Samson down on the battlefield, so he brought him down in the bedroom. It was a sneak attack through this woman Delilah, whose name, ironically, means "delicate." She began to break down Samson's resolve and resistance until he finally confessed to her the secret of his supernatural strength (see Judges 16:16–21). If only he could have come to his senses and realized he was falling into a trap.

It is the same thing with lust. It's devastating, and it's destroying thousands of marriages today as well as ruining the lives of countless young people. It is even ending or dramatically altering lives through sexually transmitted diseases.

You might be thinking, "I really don't need to hear this. I would never fall into sin. My spouse and I have an ideal marriage. I can't imagine any circumstances in which I would ever be unfaithful." I remember listening to an interview with a man who had written some Christian books on the family. This man had boasted to his friends, "If I ever fall into sin, I guarantee it will not be adultery. Anything but. I love my wife so much that it would never happen to me." Do you know what happened? You guessed it. This man fell into the sin of adultery, and he realized the very thing that he said he would never do, he did. He concluded by saying, "An unguarded strength is a double weakness." I think that is very true.

Whenever we say things like, "I would never fall into that sin," we are on thin ice. After all, 1 Corinthians 10:12 tells us, "Therefore let him who thinks he stands take heed lest he fall." Any of us are capable of committing any sin. Believe that. Please. Don't think that somehow you are above something—that you would never fall into a certain sin. You are capable of doing the worst things. So am I. It is because "the heart is deceitful above all things, and desperately wicked..." (Jer. 17:9). As Paul says, "For I know that in me (that is, in my flesh) nothing good dwells; for to will is present with me, but how to perform what is good I do not find" (Rom. 7:18). That doesn't mean that I will do all these sinful things, but it simply means the potential is always there. If I allow temptation to infiltrate my life and my old nature to prevail, I could fall, just as surely as a fire will spread by putting gasoline on it. But if I take practical steps and precautions to guard myself and to stay close to the Lord, then I don't have to fall.

In warning believers about sexual immorality, Paul said, "Nor let us commit sexual immorality, as some of them did, and in one day twenty-three thousand fell ... " (1 Cor. 10:8). Here, Paul was referring to the Book of Numbers and the story of the greedy prophet, Balaam, who was a sort of "prophet for hire." When Balak, the king of the Moabites, wanted the Israelites defeated, he thought that finding a prophet to curse them and bring God's judgment on them would be much easier than having to defeat them on the battlefield. I don't know where he found Balaam. Maybe he looked in the Moab Yellow Pages under "profit," because that seems to be all Balaam was interested in. Whatever the case, he secured Balaam's services, told him to go and curse Israel, and offered a very generous contract to do it. Balaam said, "No problem." So he went out to curse Israel, but God spoke to Balaam and told him not to curse Israel, but to bless them.

This didn't exactly endear him to Balak. He didn't hire the prophet to bless the people; he hired him to curse them. Still, Balaam was determined to somehow find a way to get this money. He went on his way to do what God had told him not to do, and in one of the Bible's most attention-grabbing narratives, his donkey spoke to him. You would think that would have been enough for Balaam right then and there. But he persisted and eventually devised a plan. He said, "I'll tell you what, Balak. I cannot curse the Israelites. God has told me not to. But I have an idea. If you can get some of your young, sensual Moabite women to sexually entice these young Israelite men to go into their tents and have sexual relations with them, that is a way you can get them to worship the false gods. If these Israelite men actually go into the tents and engage in this idolatry, this will bring God's wrath on the people and He will judge them."

Balak said, "Good idea," and he enlisted the women to do the work. So the young women went out, and it was a success—depending on how you look at it. The story is recorded in Numbers 25, where we read,

> Now Israel remained in Acacia Grove, and the people began to commit harlotry with the women of Moab. They invited the people to the sacrifices of their gods, and the people ate and bowed down to their gods. So Israel was joined to Baal of Peor, and the anger of the Lord was aroused against Israel. Then the Lord said to Moses, "Take all the leaders of the people and hang the offenders before the Lord, out in the sun, that the fierce anger of the Lord may turn away from Israel." (vv. 1–4)

These were not the first people to be destroyed by immorality, and they won't be the last. So Paul was now bringing this example before the people he was speaking to: the church of Corinth and to believers who are living in the last days. The Corinthian believers were a bit smug. They somehow thought they would never fall into sexual sin or idolatry. This is why Paul framed these words in the way he did.

Ironically, immorality was rampant in Corinth in Paul's day. In fact, towering above the ruins of old Corinth is a 2,000-foot mountain fortress called Acrocorinth. Situated at the top of that mountain was the temple of Aphrodite, the goddess of fertility, and as many as one thousand priestesses, or prostitutes, working for the temple carried on their immoral activities in the worship of this pagan deity. It is said that prostitutes from this temple would go into the city of Corinth wearing specially designed sandals that left these words imprinted on the sand: "Follow me." Many citizens of Corinth did just that. They followed the prostitutes to the temple and committed sexual immorality as well as idolatry. I think the same invitation to commit sexual immorality is being extended to us today by way of the media's constant bombardment of our culture with sex. The message is hard to miss: "Follow me."

WATCH YOUR STEP

Usually the steps that lead to sexual immorality, including adultery, are numerous. It happens over a period of time, generally starting in the area of the imagination, and then leading up to the act itself.

We see this in the life of one man who committed adultery and paid the price for it in the years to come. His name was David. Sadly, when you think of David's life, two names come up that sum up his whole story: David and Goliath, and David and Bathsheba. One represents his greatest triumph, while the other represents his greatest defeat.

The story of David and Bathsheba is known to most. It all happened when the kings were going out to battle, and David was taking some time off, the Bible tells us. He was out strolling on his patio when he looked down and saw a beautiful woman named Bathsheba bathing herself. Now, he couldn't have avoided that first look—and sometimes you wonder if Bathsheba allowed herself to be in a place where she would be seen by David, knowing perhaps she was within view. I don't know. But the Bible never points the finger at her. David was the culprit in this case. He couldn't have avoided that first look, but the second one is probably what got him into trouble.

He then began to devise a plan in which he could have Bathsheba. Misusing his authority and position as king, he commanded Bathsheba to be brought up to his chambers. He had sexual relations with her, and Bathsheba became pregnant. But instead of confessing his sin to God, he tried to cover up what he had done. So he sent word that Bathsheba's husband, Uriah, who was serving David in his army, was to be brought back to be with his wife. David wanted to cover it up.

Uriah was brought back, but David hadn't counted on the fact that Uriah was such a valiant and loyal subject that he could not bear to have the pleasure of being with his wife when his fellow soldiers were out risking their lives. So he slept outside his own house that night. David should have stopped right there. It was as though God was putting an obstacle in his path, trying to warn him. But David persisted. He got Uriah drunk, then sent him in to be with his wife. Again, Uriah would not have relations with his wife.

So David ordered his commander to have Uriah sent to the front lines, where he was killed in the heat of battle. Then, without wasting much time, David took Bathsheba into his home and married her.

David may have thought he pulled it off, but it doesn't work that way. The Bible says, "He who covers his sins will not prosper" (Prov. 28:13). For twelve months, David lived out of harmony and fellowship with the God he loved so much. He wrote in the psalms about what it is like to live out of fellowship with God when there is unconfessed sin, and his words still ring so true to any who have ever been in a similar position: "When I kept silent, my bones grew old through my groaning all the day long. For day and night Your hand was heavy upon me; my vitality was turned into the drought of summer" (Psalm 32:3–4).

If you are engaged in unconfessed sin right now, be it in action or even in the realm of the imagination, then you know what David is talking about. You know the destruction that that sin can bring. That is why the Bible tells us in Proverbs 6:32, "But the man who commits adultery is an utter fool, for he destroys his own soul" (NLT). If you choose to commit adultery, then you are choosing self-destruction.

IT WILL COST YOU

Considering how widespread this sin is, we need to just think about its repercussions and count the cost, because the cost is great. I want to give you a number of reasons as to why you should not be unfaithful to your spouse:

Reason one: You do incredible damage to your spouse. Paul wrote, "And don't you know that if a man joins himself to a prostitute, he becomes one body with her? For the Scriptures say, 'The two are united into one' " (1 Cor. 6:16 NLT). You might call it a one-night fling when you are involved sexually with someone beside your spouse. You may say it didn't mean anything. But I will tell you that it means a lot. It means more than you will ever know, because you have violated that bond that you have with your spouse. That is why Jesus gave a release clause from the marriage because of the sin of adultery, because it violates the very fiber of the marriage (see Matt. 5:32). It strikes at the very foundation. That is not to say there isn't forgiveness, and that isn't to say you can't recover from it. I know of couples who have, but it still is difficult and painful in the process.

But I could also share with you many cases where adultery was committed and the marriages fell apart, because usually adultery is not a one-night fling or a one-night stand. Usually it is a series of steps that are taken that required habitual deception and lying, and these often can be as devastating to a spouse as the act itself.

Reason two: You damage yourself. To get into this place, it means that you have had to harden yourself against God, and in essence, you have been in a backslidden state. That is hurting you spiritually. Not only that, you put yourself at risk physically. There is something called AIDS that is a potential problem with any person who is sexually immoral in this culture. That is not to imply that every person who has AIDS has been sexually immoral. But I do think one of the biggest myths that has been propagated, especially among our nation's youth, is the concept of "safe sex." It is a blatant lie. I could cite statistic after statistic about how it isn't safe and how there is a great risk factor involved.

A few years ago, I spoke with an individual who had come to our church for counseling. He was terrified because he had been unfaithful to his wife on many occasions and thought he had AIDS. He had been tested and was waiting for the results. He had to go home and tell his wife what he had done. He put her at risk while he was out fooling around. What a tragedy.

People don't think clearly when they are hooked by lust and sexual sin, do they? That is why the Bible warns us to stay away from it because of its deceptive allure and the power it can exercise over our minds.

It reminds me of a news story I read about a man who lived in England. He had a pet scorpion, which he named Twiggy. Apparently, this man would kiss his pet scorpion goodnight. Each night, he would take Twiggy in his hand and give it a little kiss. One night, to his total surprise, his little pet scorpion stung him on the lip. When the man opened his mouth in shock, the scorpion jumped in and stung him again. Two things came to mind when I read that story. I won't tell you what the first thing was, because it wouldn't be kind. But the second thing I thought of was that this man underestimated the nature of that creature.

In the same way, we will commit, in our estimation, a "little" sin—something that we don't think is significant. Then we're shocked when it turns around and bites us. We're shocked when it hurts us. We can't believe it happened.

Reason three: You damage your children. By his own hand, a man dramatically undermines his position as spiritual leader in the home if he commits adultery. His children's trust in him has been eroded, not to mention the trust of his wife. Children may, in turn, even repeat the same sin. How can you tell your children to be sexually pure when mom or dad has gone out and had an affair? I remember hearing about one teenage girl who had been sexually promiscuous, and when her dad confronted her about it, she said, "Well, Dad, you did it. What's the big deal?" He had been involved in an affair not long before that.

God forgave David of his sin of adultery, but he still paid the price for years to come. David's son, Amnon, raped his half-sister, Tamar. Then another son, Absalom, killed Amnon. So two sins that David himself had committed, sexual immorality and murder, were also committed by his children. Your children will look at your example.

Reason four: You damage the church. Scripture teaches that when one member suffers, the whole body suffers (see 1 Corinthians 12:26). As believers, we are interconnected. The victories and defeats of individuals affect the body as a whole. That is why Paul told the believers in Corinth who had a sexually immoral man in their midst to remove him from their fellowship. He told them, "A little leaven leavens the whole lump" (1 Cor. 5:6). Once that man had repented, he was readmitted into the fellowship of the church. But prior to that, Paul told them not to tolerate that kind of thing in their ranks. It's like a cancer. It spreads and destroys the integrity and effectiveness of the church.

Reason five: You do great damage to your witness and to the cause of Christ. As the prophet Nathan said to David after he had sinned, "By this deed you have given great occasion to the enemies of the Lord to blaspheme" (2 Sam. 12:14). It is one more thing for unbelievers to hang their doubts on.

Reason six: You sin against the Lord. This should be the primary reason we avoid sin, but sadly, it is usually the last thing we even consider. I think what is lacking in the hearts of many Christians today is the fear of God. By "the fear of God," I don't mean the fear of righteous retribution, but the fear of displeasing Him. One of the best definitions of the fear of God that I have heard is, "A wholesome dread of displeasing Him." In other words, you love God so much that you don't want to do something that would displease Him and bring shame to His name and to the cause of Christ.

Joseph had it right when he was tempted by Potiphar's wife and replied, "How then can I do this great wickedness, and sin against God?" (Gen. 39:9). Joseph didn't say, "What if your husband walks in? He will kill me!" Or, "It could ruin my career!" Those weren't his considerations. He didn't want to sin against the Lord. That is the highest motive of all. All other motives should just be reinforcements.

DON'T LET IT HAPPEN TO YOU

So what steps can we take to prevent this devastating sin of sexual immorality? What can we do to build a wall of protection around our lives and around our marriages?

Walk with God. It's simple, but true. If a husband or wife is truly walking with God, it will give him or her the power to stand strong against temptation and say, like Joseph, "How then can I do this great wickedness, and sin against God?" It was David's failure to do this that made him vulnerable to the temptations he faced.

Job said, "I have made a covenant with my eyes; why then should I look upon a young woman?" (Job 31:1). Job said. "I am guarding myself. I am careful as to what I look at." On the same subject, Jesus said,

> "You have heard that it was said to those of old, 'You shall not commit adultery.' But I say to you that whoever looks at a woman to lust for her has already committed adultery with her in his heart. If your right eye causes you to sin, pluck it out and cast it from you; for it is more profitable for you that one of your members perish, than for your whole body to be cast into hell."
> (Matt. 5:27–29)

When Jesus used the phrase, "looks at a woman," He wasn't just talking about seeing her. Jesus was not even talking about being exposed to something you did not want to be exposed to. Sometimes we cannot control our environment and what is thrown in front of us, and sometimes we can. Jesus wasn't talking about a casual glance. Rather, He was referring to a continual act of looking. In this usage, the idea is not of an incidental or involuntarily glance, but an intentional and repeated gazing with the express purpose of lusting. I might also add that this statement doesn't apply to men only. It also applies to women looking lustfully at men. So what this refers to here is a person who is going out of his or her way to look at someone to lust after them. They are looking at someone for the deliberate purpose of lusting.

So here was Jesus' solution: "If your right eye causes you to sin, pluck it out and cast it from you." Of course, if we took this literally, there wouldn't be many people left with their right eye. Obviously Jesus was not speaking literally, because if you pluck out your right eye, you could still lust with your left. So we need to understand the culture of the time, which is often helpful in interpreting various passages of Scripture. In the Jewish culture, the right hand represented a person's best and most precious faculties, and the right eye represented one's best vision. What Jesus was saying, in essence, is that you should be willing to give up whatever is necessary to keep from falling into sin. Whatever steps you have to take that would prevent you from falling morally or spiritually, take them.

If there is something in your life, whether it's a relationship or something you are doing that is causing you to commit this sin of looking with lust, then you need to stop. Now. Looking always leads to doing. If it is not stopped at some point, then sooner or later, you will be tired of just looking and you will want to start doing. That is why it needs to be nipped in the bud—in the realm of your mind.

The Bible says, "Walk in the Spirit, and you shall not fulfill the lust of the flesh" (Gal. 5:16). The best defense is a good offense. So walk with God.

Walk with your spouse. In other words, enjoy a close and intimate friendship and romance with your wife or husband. Remember at very foundation of a marriage, and what is missing in many marriages, is that a husband and wife should be companions and friends. I can't emphasize this enough: your wife or your husband should be your best friend. And then, keep the romance alive in your marriage. Cultivate it. If the romance is dying, then get back and throw some more logs on the fire. Do what you can to rekindle it again. Sexually fulfill each other. The Bible tells you, "Drink water from your own cistern, and running water from your own well" (Prov. 5:15). Find fulfillment in your marriage relationship as husband and wife, as God has created you and has blessed that union.

Don't walk in the counsel of the ungodly. Avoid, at all costs, any relationship or friendship that could cause you to fall.

If you are in that kind of relationship with someone of the

opposite sex right now, if you're flirting and playing around, then it's time to throw on the brakes. "Oh, it's innocent," you might say. Listen. You never know what it can lead to. Avoid it at all costs. Avoid even the appearance of evil.

Count the cost. Remember some of the warnings we've been looking at. These, along with an intense love for God and your spouse, can see you through the rough waters of sexual temptation.

Temptation will be around as long as we live. But we don't have to fall into it if we take the steps God has given us. And if you have fallen into it, stop. Repent. Don't continue in it. Thank God there is forgiveness, and learn from your mistakes.

Let's not forget the words of 1 Corinthians 10:13, "No temptation has overtaken you except such as is common to man; but God is faithful, who will not allow you to be tempted beyond what you are able, but with the temptation will also make the way of escape, that you may be able to bear it." This clearly tells us that God won't give us more than we can handle. He won't let us be tempted above our capacity to resist. So you don't have to give in to that impure thought. You don't have to give in to that idea.

You know you can't stop yourself from being tempted. But remember, the tempter needs cooperation with the temptee. We are tempted, the Bible says, when we are drawn away by our own lusts and enticed (see James 1:14). So while it is true that temptation can be strong, you still must be willing to cooperate with it in order to sin.

As it has been said, you can't stop a bird from flying over your head, but you can stop it from building a nest in your hair. It is not a sin to be tempted. Jesus was tempted, after all. But it is a sin to give in to temptation. You have a choice in the matter.

STRENGTH TRAINING

- *Ask God to reveal to you any activities or relationships you're presently engaged in that could be potentially harmful to you and your spouse. Then do what you need to do to remove them from your life today.*

DAILY SUPPLEMENTS

- *Each day this week, read one of the following selections from* Marriage Connections: *"Avoid Temptation," "A Time to Run," "Plow Your Own Field," "Serious Business," "Make Room for Forgiveness," "Standing Firm in the Firestorm," and "Choose the Right Path."*

*Many waters cannot quench love; neither can
rivers drown it. If a man tried to buy love
with everything he owned, his offer would be
utterly despised. (Song of Solomon 8:7 NLT)*

MARRIAGE IS A LIFELONG LIFESTYLE

A pastor went to speak to a group of fourth graders on the topic of marriage. As the children gathered together, he said, "Kids, I want to talk to you about marriage today. I wonder if any of you could tell me what God has to say about marriage." Immediately one little boy waved his hand back and forth, so the pastor called on him and said, "OK son, what does God say about marriage?"

The little boy replied, "Father, forgive them, for they know not what they do."

There are a lot of miserable people out there who have not found their marriages to be what they had expected. Maybe that is why one person said, "Marriage is like a three-ring circus: engagement ring, wedding ring, and suffering." If that is a description of your marriage right now, I want you to know that it can change.

By God's grace, I have had the privilege of being married to Cathe for thirty-two years now. We thank the Lord for that. Prior to getting married, we courted for three years. We wanted to really get to know each other. Apparently we were following the advice of Benjamin Franklin, who said, "Keep your eyes wide open before marriage and half shut afterward." I wanted to know what I was getting, and I'm sure that Cathe wanted to know what she was getting as well. We had some pretty dramatic disagreements and arguments during those three years. We also had big break-ups. In fact, we broke up three times while we were courting. It basically became an annual event. But after we spent time apart from each other, we realized were meant to be together. We realized we really loved each other. Instead of our love diminishing over the passing of time, it only grew stronger.

It has been said, "Love at first sight is nothing special. It's when people have been looking at each other for years that it becomes a miracle." We have been looking at each other for years now, and Cathe looks more beautiful every year. My friend Franklin Graham says that each Christmas when he receives a photograph of our family, it's as though Cathe is frozen in time and I am in an accelerated phase of aging. I'm just glad that no one has mistaken her for my daughter yet.

I was 21 and Cathe was 18 when we were married, and I can remember that day like yesterday. She was a vision as she came down that aisle radiantly dressed in white. There was a shaft of light coming through the window that shone through her veil; it was as though she was almost illuminated. I, on the other hand, basically looked like Grizzly Adams, with long, blonde hair and a big red beard. Cathe tells me the same shaft of light I saw coming through her veil was also shining on my beard, which looked to her like a bright-red burning bush. But Cathe saw something in me underneath all of that hair (basically, a bald man waiting to emerge).

We established our marriage on some biblical principles, and we are still following those same principles today. While I am certainly not an expert on marriage, I do know a little bit about marriage and divorce, because I have experienced both. I came from a divorced home. I had five different men in my life that were fathers, if you could call them that. So, I know what it is like to be raised in a broken home. I know what it is like to experience the pain that divorce can bring into a person's life. Maybe that is one of the reasons I have such distaste for divorce and want to do everything I can to move married couples away from that direction if they might be considering it.

A STRONG MARRIAGE IS NO ACCIDENT

Tragically, we are living in a time in which a family that stays together is becoming more and more of a rarity. And a flourishing marriage? Well, that's a downright oddity. But it doesn't have to be that way. God can bless your marriage, and in fact, that is what He wants to do. After all, let's remember that God invented marriage. He knows how it should function. Therefore, we must find those principles given to us in Scripture, and we must follow them. I can say, without any hesitation, that next to salvation itself, a marriage lived out according to God's design is the most fulfilling and wonderful thing that I know on this earth. That is why Proverbs 18:22 says, "The man who finds a wife finds a treasure and receives favor from the Lord" (NLT). As the saying goes, "Marriage halves our griefs, doubles our joys, and it quadruples our expenses." But it is worth every penny.

A strong and happy marriage is not only fulfilling spiritually, but it even benefits you emotionally as well. Research has actually shown that people who are married live longer than people who are not. They go to doctors less often. They make less use of other health care services. Virtually every study of mortality and marital status show that the unmarried of both sexes have higher death rates, whether by accident, disease, or self-inflicted wounds. In fact, records dating back to the nineteenth century show that the highest suicide rates occur among the divorced, followed by widows and widowers, and those who never married. The lowest rates of suicide were among people who were married.

Even with all of its benefits, marriage has not been a happy experience for everyone. J. Paul Getty, one of the wealthiest men who ever lived said, "I would give my entire fortune for one happy marriage." That is a tragic statement, isn't it? If you have a happy marriage today, then you have more than one of the world's wealthiest men ever had.

Yet having a strong and healthy marriage is no accident. It takes hard work. Yet some people spend more time planning for a wedding than they do for marriage. Some people will put more effort into what they will be wearing for a few hours on their wedding day than they how they will live and function for the rest of their married lives.

Many of us probably remember the wedding day of Prince Charles, the Prince of Wales, to Lady Diana Spencer on July

29, 1981. London was dressed like a vast stage. There were flowers everywhere. With great pomp and circumstance, Lady Diana and Prince Charles rode in royal carriages to the magnificent St. Paul's Cathedral. They recited their marriage vows to one another in the presence of the queen, along with many VIPs and foreign dignitaries from around the world. The fairytale-like event was broadcast to a global audience of 750 million people. On that picture-perfect day, it would have been almost impossible to imagine the adversity that awaited this royal couple, from their highly publicized divorce to Diana's tragic death in 1997. Other than their two sons, basically all that remains of that union is tabloid fodder.

THE AGE OF DRIVE-THROUGH DIVORCE

We have all heard the phrase, "a marriage made in heaven," which almost implies that some marriages simply work out and some don't. It as if to say, "Hopefully your marriage will be one of those made in heaven. But if it isn't, then it's no problem. Just bail out. It doesn't matter. You will do better next time." Meanwhile, the divorce rate continues to spiral out of control.

It is this very cavalier attitude about marriage that not only is destroying families, but is destroying the very fabric of our country. Today, the United States leads the world in the most divorces in a monogamous nation.[2] We even have such things as drive-through divorce courts. I read about one in Tampa, Florida. Meanwhile, this breakdown of the family is having a devastating impact on our nation. According to the National Fatherhood Initiative, children of divorce are "more likely to be suspended from school, or to drop out; be treated for an emotional or behavioral problem; commit suicide as adolescents; and be victims of child abuse or neglect" than the children of intact families.[3]

The problem is that we treat marriage as something disposable. What concerns me is that this same mentality has found its way into the church. I have seen far too many marriages dissolved for no good reason.

I will grant that, in a very small number of situations, it

may be true there are people who have divorced who should have divorced. But in my experience as a pastor for more than three decades, I have found that most marriages that ended in divorce did not need to. There were no biblical grounds for it. These marriages did not need to fall apart. Rather, they fell apart due to neglect and a lack of obedience regarding what the Bible says. When we tamper with God's plan, we do so at our own peril.

If you want a good marriage, you can have one. But it takes work—and lots of it. If you want a bad marriage, you can have one too—simply through neglect and letting it sort of find its own way. God has given us clear principles in His Word on how to have a strong marriage. We have reviewed a number of them in this book. Now we have to ask God to enable us to obey Him, through the help of His Holy Spirit.

BUILD ON THE RIGHT FOUNDATION

Marriage is a lot like a mirror. It gives back a reflection of you. Many times, I don't like mirrors. They show me something I don't want to see, especially in the morning. It's a frightening thing to see your own reflection sometimes. When it comes to your marriage, you make it into what it is. If you don't like what you are seeing in the marital mirror, so to speak, then it's time to do something about it.

We have to get back to God's plan and God's principles. These principles haven't been given to some imaginary spiritual elite, but to ordinary people like you and me—people who live in this real world and face real challenges. In addition to everything else, the Bible is a practical book. Not only is it the inspired Word of God, but it is also a book that speaks to real life. It tells us how to live.

Jesus said, "Therefore whoever hears these sayings of Mine, and does them, I will liken him to a wise man who built his house on the rock: and the rain descended, the floods came, and the winds blew and beat on that house; and it did not fall, for it was founded on the rock" (Matt. 7:24–25). Storms will come into every life. As it has been said, into every life a little rain must fall. In some lives, a lot of rain falls. Sometimes it even hails, and there is thunder and light-ening. In the same way, every marriage will encounter storms. But if your marriage is built on a solid foundation, you will be able to come through the storms stronger as a result. But if your marriage is built on a weak foundation of sand, symbol-izing those who hear the Word and don't obey it, then those storms will devastate you. It is a whole lot easier to lay the foundation right the first time and build on it than it is to redo a foundation while you are living in the house.

I have never built a house, but I have remodeled. People who have built their houses have told me that it is much easier to build than to remodel. Maybe you will have to do a little remodeling of your marriage. It will be hard. But it is better than the alternative, which is having your marriage fall apart. I think a good place for Christians to begin in their effort to have a healthy and strong marriage is to strike the word, "divorce," from their vocabularies.

Of course, I'm aware the Bible gives certain grounds for divorce. I recognize there are situations where it is justified and understandable. But again, I want to emphasize that the vast majority of divorces today do not have to happen. Because we tend to view divorce as an escape hatch, we use it far too readily. Instead, we need to say, "We are not even going to consider that as an option. We are going to honor our vows, which were for better or for worse, for richer or poorer, in sickness and health, to love and to cherish, until death do us part." If you have made these vows, you can keep them with the help and the power of God. (If you are single and reading this today, let me just say that if you are not willing to keep these vows, don't ever get married.) It is time to turn the tide.

"VICTORY IS NOT WON BY EVACUATION"

You might be thinking, "It's too late. You can't turn back time." Maybe not, but I am reminded of the question, "How do you eat an elephant?" The answer is, "One bite at a time." In the same way, how do we turn this trend back? One bite at a time. If every couple would say, "This is not going to happen in our home. We are going to draw the line right here. We are going to make our stand," then we will have taken quite a few bites together.

During World War II when England was bombarded nightly by the Nazis, the people of that country began to despair. They wanted Prime Minister Winston Churchill to surrender. But he refused. Then he made this statement: "Victory is not won by evacuation." You can apply that same truth to marriage. Victory is not won by evacuation. We must determine to persevere.

We have looked at God's order for the man and the woman in marriage. We have looked at God's objective in bringing the woman to the man: to make him a helper, or literally, someone who corresponds to him. This phrase is used elsewhere in the Old Testament in reference to someone who comes to rescue another. So Eve came to rescue Adam from loneliness. She came to bring completion and fulfillment in his life. She would provide what had been missing in his life up to this point.

We have looked at God's principle of leaving and cleaving, which sums up the foundation of all teaching on marriage. Marriage begins with the leaving, which means leaving all other relationships. This doesn't mean that you sever all relationships, but it does mean they are altered—they are changed as a result of marriage. Family and friends have their place. But your best friend, your closest friend, should be your spouse. In fact, it is really what a marriage is built on. Sexual intimacy is part of the marriage relationship and is the only place where it can be expressed in a meaningful way that is pleasing and acceptable to God. But that is not what a marriage is built on. Those who have been married for a period of time would offer a hearty "amen" to that statement. Marriage is built on friendship, and so it should be.

Yet in all too many marriages today, friendship has been lost. The husband and wife are still lovers. They see themselves as parents to their children and maybe even partners in their own little enterprise. But they have forgotten what it is like to be friends. They have forgotten what it's like to bare their hearts and to share their souls. They have forgotten to keep one another updated on what is going on in their lives. It begins to affect everything else in their relationship, and they begin to drift apart.

Malachi 2:14 says, " 'The Lord has been witness between you and the wife of your youth, with whom you have dealt treacherously; yet she is your companion and your wife by covenant.' " The word used here for "companion" means, "one you are united with in thoughts, goals, plans, and efforts."

Husband, are you united with your wife in thoughts, goals, plans, and efforts? I would suspect that your wife would love to have a close friendship with you. But I would also suspect that you might be the one who isn't doing much of the communicating. That needs to change. You need to know what your wife loves, what she is afraid of, what her greatest hope is, as well as her greatest fear. How well do you know her? Do you know her favorite color or her favorite song? What is her favorite restaurant?

The thing is, we change over the passing of time. Cathe is not the same person she was when I married her. I am not the same person I was when she married me. We both have changed over the years. Hopefully, we have become stronger in our faith. Hopefully, we have deepened in who we are. I know that my wife has, and I hope that I have as well. It is a constant process of learning about and knowing the person you are married to.

This leads us to the second half of this foundational marriage principle, which is cleaving. We learned that the word, "cleave," speaks of sticking together. It doesn't mean being stuck together, but sticking together. God wants you to be glued to your spouse—not stuck, but glued, because you want to be. You hold on to each other. You want to strengthen the ties that bind. You want to do what you can to keep the relationship strong.

So we must periodically ask ourselves as husbands and wives, "Are we doing what it takes to strengthen our relationship? Are we engaged in any relationship or pursuit that could potentially put distance between our mate and ourselves? Will this thing that we are doing right now drive us apart or will it pull us together? Will it build our relationship or will it tear it down? Are we leaving and cleaving?" Ask yourselves these questions. It's basic, but it's essential.

Lots of people today have gone through the process of leaving, but they are not cleaving. Others have failed to both leave and cleave. They have closer relationships with their friends than with their own spouse. It's time to change. It's time to get back to God's original plan. Remember, marriage is based first and foremost on friendship and closeness and intimacy.

So rekindle that fire in your home. It isn't some mystical thing that is impossible to do. Imagine sitting in your living room and when the fire begins to die down, you say, "That's it. That fire is gone. We will never have another fire again. It was a great fire, but I guess now it's time to get a new house and a new fireplace." That sounds ridiculous. But that is what some couples do. Instead, they just needed to throw another log on the fire. It will keep that marriage fire going.

But how do you that? How do you rekindle the fire? The logs I'm speaking of are the practical steps you take toward building a stronger marriage. We've looked at some of them here. We've learned what they are. So now it's time to get moving.

STRENGTH TRAINING

- *Skim through this and the previous chapters. Has God spoken to you about something in your marriage that needs to change? Take a moment to write it down in a place where you can go back to it, such as in the space below. Then, ask God to help you make that change and commit to doing your part in helping your marriage become all that God intended it to be.*

DAILY SUPPLEMENTS

- *Each day this week, read one of the following selections from* Marriage Connections: *"Building on the Rock," "No Accident," "Imitate God," "Spend Time with the Godly," "An Act of Patriotism," "The Secret to Love," and "Leaving a Spiritual Legacy."*

NOTES

1. Dr. James C. Dobson, *Love for a Lifetime* (Portland, Ore.: Multnomah Press, 1987), 42–43.
2. *Guinness World Records*, accessed November 15, 2004: available at http://www.guinnessworldrecords.com.
3. Roland Warren, *National Fatherhood Initiative*, accessed November 16, 2004: available at http://www.fatherhood.org/ prezwel.asp.

OTHER ALLENDAVID BOOKS
PUBLISHED BY KERYGMA PUBLISHING

*The Great
Compromise*

*For Every Season:
Daily Devotions*

*Marriage
Connections*

*Are We Living
in the Last Days?*

Visit:

www.kerygmapublishing.com
www.allendavidbooks.com
www.harvest.org